"Chris Williams is a survivor and his memoir is nothing less than survival manual for those struggling with their own inexplicable suffering. His poignant words pulsate with pain and at the same time, astonishingly, testify to hope beyond unspeakable loss, the possibility that one can somehow get through the worst of times. For this we are deeply indebted to the author!"

—Louis Stulman
author of *Order Amid Chaos*

"In his book, Williams masterfully invites us deep into the recesses of suffering ... using Jeremiah and his own story as a backdrop for hope, understanding, and even appreciation for the valleys we travel. This book is a tremendous guide for all who have, will, or continue to walk through the shadows of suffering."

—Don Schiewer Jr.
Pastor, New Harvest Christian Church

Life After Suffering

Life After Suffering
A Memoir of Subversive Hope

CHRIS WILLIAMS

Foreword by Benji Ballmer

WIPF & STOCK · Eugene, Oregon

LIFE AFTER SUFFERING
A Memoir of Subversive Hope

Copyright © 2011 Chris Williams. All rights reserved. Except for brief quotations in critical publications or reviews, no part of this book may be reproduced in any manner without prior written permission from the publisher. Write: Permissions, Wipf and Stock Publishers, 199 W. 8th Ave., Suite 3, Eugene, OR 97401.

All scripture quotations, unless otherwise indicated, are taken from the Holy Bible, Today's New International Version®. TNIV®. Copyright © 2001, 2005 by Biblica, Inc.™ Used by permission of Zondervan. All rights reserved worldwide. www.zondervan.com

Quotation from Nicholas Wolterstorff, *Lament for a Son* (Grand Rapids: Eerdmans, 1987) on page 108–9 reprinted with permission of William B. Eerdmans Publishing Company.

Wipf & Stock
An Imprint of Wipf and Stock Publishers
199 W. 8th Ave., Suite 3
Eugene, OR 97401

www. wipfandstock.com

ISBN 13: 978-1-60608-701-5

Manufactured in the U.S.A.

For Christi

וַיֶּאֱהָבֶהָ וַיִּנָּחֵם יִצְחָק אַחֲרֵי אִמּוֹ

Contents

Foreword / xi

Before We Begin . . . / 1

Movement 1: Death and All His Friends
1 Coming Out of the Garage / 11
2 Irrevocable Loss / 31

Movement 2: The Moment of Inescapable Waiting
3 Black Thursday / 51
4 Weeping Alone . . . Together / 68
5 Suffering With / 88

Movement 3: A New Song to Sing
6 Hope Arising / 110
7 Judah's New Song / 129

Conclusion / 146

Acknowledgments / 149
Bibliography / 151
Contact the Author / 153

Foreword

Reader Beware:

The contents of the following pages are not for the faint of heart. If you are happy with your faith, journey, and view of God, then proceed no further.

If you have scheduled your life around avoiding the truth, skirting suffering, and turning a blind eye to the scary and sad stories of this world, then this book is not for you ... or maybe it is especially for you.

Perhaps you have been trained, as I was, to read the story of the scriptures through a lens that paints the Bible as safe for the whole family and rated at most ... PG (parental guidance suggested). After reading this book you might see that perhaps it deserves an R rating, and we would actually not be able to admit anyone under the age of 18 unless accompanied by an adult. If this makes you uncomfortable, then think twice before proceeding.

Or maybe you are wondering if you have screwed up somewhere along the way and perhaps you have done something terribly wrong to deserve the torture that you went through, or are currently going through. Maybe you deserve the abandonment that you feel, the pain that you harbor, the disillusionment with your life, your relationships, perhaps even God and/or the church. Or it could be that you have experienced suffering, walked through it and out to the other side and wonder if you are the only one who has felt the things you feel, or sees things the way you now see them.

In other words, the following pages will either really screw you up or really straighten you out. They have done both to me and I will continue to be both pulled and prodded, tried and tested, affirmed and built up by the content within. This is, after all, the story we find ourselves in. If you have lived, you have suffered. If by some set of circumstances you have not yet suffered, trust me, you will.

For most of my life, I was not forced to suffer. I have not experienced the death of a loved one. I did not have a disease or seen someone I loved with a disease. I felt no pain, agony, or depression and was convinced somehow that it was because I was walking with God properly and that if only everyone could also do this, they would experience the same. The only part of scripture that I saw were the parts that spoke of joy, blessings, and the general flowing of milk and honey.

Fortunately, and I am careful to use that word, things did not stay that way for me. My individual story is only important as far as it pertains to how I met the author of this book and how his own story and questions helped me to form mine. Notice I said *nothing* about ANSWERS...

Benjamin J. Ballmer
fellow sojourner

Before We Begin . . .

I CAN STILL FEEL my daddy's arms wrapped around me as I sat on his lap for story time. Those arms were rough and strong but at the same time they comforted my little boy body to the depths of my little boy bones. And I can still hear the sweet voice of my mommy as she took the words on the page and brought them to my imagination night after night. Those memories of story time as a child remain one of my favorite companions as I find myself farther along the journey of life.

There was this one story that was a favorite. It was about a tree and a boy, and this particular story had a way of drawing me into it to where I could feel the bark of the tree on my fingers, taste its apples, hear its leaves rustling.

You know that feeling?

Well, as the story goes, this tree gave to the boy, and gave, and gave, and gave until it had sacrificed all it was for the sake of the boy,[1] and after my mom or dad read the final "The End" I knew in my little boy mind that something I just heard was true.

Maybe giving for the sake of others was the best way to live.

Maybe there's something about sacrifice that is innately compelling.

Maybe that story was true.

But it was just a story, and adults everywhere made sure I knew that trees didn't really talk.

That's the beauty of story, it's also the mystery of story. Story can take many forms, but often stories are shared by grouping words together, and if done well then that grouping of words becomes much more than just a grouping of words. It becomes alive. It moves and breathes. It becomes, dare I say, something true. I'm not just talking about intellectual truth. I'm talking about the moments in life when we are provoked to use words like good, just, right, and beautiful.

---

1. Silverstein, *The Giving Tree*.

My children and I were recently reenacting this storytelling experience from my childhood, except this time it was my arms and my voice. The great mystic and poet Dr. Seuss was sharing a story with us about an elephant who talked to a dust speck that was more than a dust speck, it was a world populated by beings so infinitesimally small that only the elephant could hear them. Using the best elephant voice and the best selfishly mean kangaroo voice I could, we made our way through the story until we arrived at the theme, "A person's a person. No matter how small."[2] My son's eyes found mine, and he questioned, "Dad, is that true?"

But it's just a story . . .

BILLIONS OF STORIES, ONE PLANET

Everyone has a story to tell, everyone. From the birth of humanity until the moment of our most recent breath, story is one of the threads that binds us all together. No matter what geographic location we find ourselves in, no matter what time period, story is always there. Whether I open my eyes and see the unexplainable beauty of the Andes Mountains, or whether my breakfast table is a dirt floor in East Africa, whether the Babylonian empire rules the world in my lifetime, or the American empire rules the world in my lifetime, everyone, everywhere, at every time has a story to tell.

This just happens to be mine.

Mine is like billions of others. It has characters (both heroes and villains), plot, setting, crisis moments, and moments of dénouement (yeah, thank the French for that word), moments of intense grief, and moments of speechless utopia. It is full of all the same themes: love, rejection, hope, despair, life, and death. In the end, mine isn't all that unique.

But it is unique. My crisis moments are mine and not yours. My moments of ecstasy are different than your moments of ecstasy. The way I have navigated through this exhilarating, yet confusing, journey called life is different than the way you have, and I guess I believe that by telling my story it can actually add to yours.

Isn't that the point of stories? They are meant to be shared. I need to hear the stories of others. I need to hear my friend Drew tell me about his battle with addictions throughout his life and how his wounds from his parents' divorce aren't going to bleed forever. I need Benji to share

---

2. Geisel, *Horton Hears a Who*.

with me about his experience of living in a tent in Montana for months at a time. I need Chrissy to tell me about the loneliness she felt growing up, which still affects her today. I need to hear Don express the struggles he's gone through at different times as he's sought to live out his vocational passions. Because I don't just hear those stories, I invite them into who I am. I give them permission to walk around inside of my being, and sometimes they take up residence. This isn't true of all stories. Some stories, because of my wounds, fears, or some other reason, I keep as far away from me as possible. But some stories change me, because stories have a way of doing that.

ALL THE WORLD IS A STORY

But stories aren't just confined to pages or voices. The way you and I see the world, attempt to understand it, try to make sense of it, all has to do with the story we choose to live within. Life for you and me is filled with characters, settings, plots, ironies, moments of climax (graduation, marriage, birth of a child), and moments of despair (broken relationships, failures, death of loved ones), and at some point you and I have to decide how to make sense of it all. Philosophers refer to this concept as our worldview, how we make sense of the world in which we find ourselves. In reality our worldview is simply our expression of the story we choose to live within. Everyone has a worldview, everyone lives within a story.[3] Being aware of the story we choose to live within is evidence of maturity.

Since the beginning of humanity people have been trying to convince others that their story is better than someone else's story. This can look as simple as having conversation with someone, or it can be as complicated as going to war with another nation. Everybody wants to believe that the way they see the world is the best possible way of seeing the world. This is why the world rarely ever sees moments of extended peace, because given enough resources and enough weapons I will convince people to see the world the way I see it (which often equals tilting the scales in my favor) ... or else. It takes just a short stroll through the pages of history to recognize that when one person asserts

---

3. I find J. Richard Middleton and Brian Walsh's discussion on worldview incredibly helpful in their book *The Transforming Vision: Shaping a Christian Worldview*. They suggest four questions that help one to articulate their worldview on page 35 of that book.

their "rightness" over someone else's "wrongness," great problems arise. The most horrid atrocities within our human story can all be traced to this arrogance of rightness: the Holocaust, the American slave trade, and Apartheid to name just a few from the not so distant past.

Instead of this arrogance of rightness, what if a group of people said enough was enough and chose to evaluate the "goodness" of a worldview not by its smooth articulation or its pristine logic, but rather by its embodiment? What if enough people decided to stop holding "worldview debates" and instead began to ask, "Does your worldview bring more life, more hope, more love to the people around you?"

I am thankful to be part of a community of people like this. A people who are fed up with "good arguments" and "sleek presentations." If the world does not get better around us, then we are living within the wrong story.

SUFFERING WELL

An irreducible part of being human is suffering. It is a part of the story that most of us want to skip over or erase, but we can't. No matter how hard we try, we just can't. To be human means that we will suffer. This reality led Viktor Frankl, an Auschwitz survivor, to make the statement, "If there is a meaning in life at all, then there must be a meaning in suffering. Suffering is an ineradicable part of life, even as fate and death. Without suffering and death human life cannot be complete."[4] I live in a culture that has taught me to avoid suffering, but what if, like Frankl, I can actually find meaning in my suffering? Not the flaky, bumper-sticker kind of meaning, but the kind of meaning that has depth; the kind of meaning that orients me towards hope; someone who brings life to people by just being around them.

This book offers a response to suffering through two stories. First, it offers my story.[5] My story is a story of suffering. It is a story of unspeakable tragedy and the long road towards, through, and to the other side of that tragedy, as well as the repetitive cycle of grief that comes with great loss. I don't pretend that my suffering is less than or greater than anyone else's experience of suffering. It is just mine. No matter your story, and

---

4. Frankl, *Man's Search For Meaning*, 88.

5. More accurately it offers a piece of my story, as I did not feel up to the task of a 30,000 page book chronicling my entire story. Not that you would even want to read that book.

Before We Begin . . .

no matter your moments of suffering, suffering has the curious ability to suffocate your hope and paralyze your life. My longing is that as I tell my story of suffering you will be able to see yourself and your suffering in my story, and that somehow in that interaction you will walk away with more life, more love, and more hope.

Hope, in its very nature, is a subversive creature. Every time we seek to define it, it pushes back with an unwilling acceptance of our definitions. It comes alive in places we don't expect, and has no problem giving the most powerful voices the middle finger. I don't pretend to have the patent on a definition for hope. As a matter of fact I have come to learn through my story that real hope cannot be defined, only experienced. My desire, in less words, is that my story of suffering may stir up within you hope that is tangible.

Second, there is a section of the Jewish/Christian scriptures that are referred to as the prophetic books.[6] One of the main characters within a number of these prophetic books is a group of people called the Judeans. They were a lot like you and me. They had symbols within their culture that gave life meaning. They had holidays to remember important historical events. There were those who had power, and those who didn't. They had stories they passed down to their children so that their children could make sense of the world in which they lived. And of course, they suffered.

Along with telling my story of suffering, I want to tell the story of these Judeans, and how they suffered. Although a number of the prophetic books recall their story of suffering, I want to focus on the book of Jeremiah, because as we will see, the story of the Judeans in the book of Jeremiah is a story of unspeakable suffering, loss, and despair. History is full of stories of those who have suffered and lived to tell about it. Maybe if we listen well, the Judeans will be able to teach us something about what it means to be human.

MOVEMENTS

Within both of these stories, I have come to see suffering as a piece of music and within this piece of music I hear three movements. These

---

6. In the Jewish tradition these books are split into two categories: 1) Former Prophets—Joshua, Judges, 1 & 2 Samuel and 1 & 2 Kings, and 2) Latter Prophets—Isaiah, Jeremiah, Ezekiel, and the book of the twelve (Hosea, Joel, Amos, Obadiah, Jonah, Micah, Nahum, Habakkuk, Zephaniah, Haggai, Zechariah, and Malachi).

three movements, when engaged intentionally, critique our culture's current advice and strategies on how to engage suffering. These movements propose a way of experiencing suffering that I feel is more healthy and authentically human than what our culture offers.

I see these movements within my story, and I see them within other stories as well. I became even more attuned to these movements of suffering when I encountered Frankl's book, *Man's Search For Meaning*. Within the first two-thirds of the book Frankl chronicles his experience in Auschwitz, the most famous of the German death camps during World War II. Using his previous psychiatric training, Frankl noticed three phases that the concentration camp prisoners experienced.[7] It was striking to me how Frankl's three phases seemed to coalesce with both the movements of suffering I observed within my experience of suffering and the Judean community's experience of suffering in the book of Jeremiah.

Those three movements of suffering form the structure that will guide our journey together on the pages ahead. *The first movement is the moment of death and loss.* This could be one event or a series of events, but the reality is the same in either case: life will never be the same as it was before. Life loses some of its meaning. Frankl aptly notes that the symptom that characterizes this first movement is shock.[8] That initial shock can quickly morph into other emotions, but it is the shock which begins these movements of suffering.

The second movement is the moment of inescapable waiting. This is the moment when the shock begins to fade and we start to realize the dark reality of the situation. This could occur days, weeks or even months following the first movement. It is at this point that we want to run far away and hide, but it does not take long to realize that the suffering we find ourselves in is inescapable. No matter how hard we try we can't get away from the pain and despair. No drug, no habit, nothing can permanently remove the pain caused by the reality of our suffering. This is the climatic movement in the experience of suffering. What will we do with that pain and despair? Will we run from our suffering or embrace its fierce reality? Will life ever feel "right" again?

The third movement is the emergence of hope amidst the suffering. This movement doesn't always become a reality for all who suffer. Why?

---

7. Frankl, *Man's Search For Meaning*, 26.
8. Ibid.

Why, like Viktor Frankl, can some find great meaning and hope in their suffering, yet some seem never to recover from the jarring effects of their suffering? Maybe the question could be asked this way: Is there life after suffering?

One metaphor used in ancient poetry to describe this third movement is music. There is this realization that life is a song, and sometimes that song is dark and confusing, but there were some ancient poets that spoke and wrote about singing a new song.[9] It was a refusal to see death and pain as having the last word, rather, these revolutionaries stood in the face of their suffering and claimed that there was another song to be sung, death filled suffering is not the end of the song, there is more to be sung.

These three movements will lead us through the two stories in front of us, my story of suffering and the story of the Judeans of the seventh–sixth century BCE. I invite you into these stories. And who knows, maybe these stories will find their way into your story.

---

9. Psalm 33:3, 40:3, 96:1, 98:1, 144:9, 149:1; Isaiah 42:10.

Movement 1

Death and All His Friends[1]

---

1. Thanks to Coldplay, specifically their *Viva La Vida (Capitol, 2008)* album, for the title of this movement.

1

Coming Out of the Garage

Utter distress has filled my soul
My life has arrived at the grave ...

—Sons of Korah
Psalm 88

"Hey mom, how are you feeling?"

"I'm ... I'm fine honey, how are finals shaping up?"

"Shouldn't be too bad, I moved my stats final so I should be able to come home Tuesday instead of Thursday," although this is the information mom is looking for, the shakiness of her voice tells me there is more going on underneath the surface. "Mom, honestly, how are you, and how is Dad?"

Her pause, along with the muted sniffle, clearly communicates to me the reality that she isn't "fine." I get the sense, on the other end of the phone, that she is going to another room to continue our conversation. When she continues I hear an all too familiar tone of voice. It is a voice of weakness, despair, and exhaustion. If I were face to face with her I would be able to see the mask of "fine" come off, and the true state of my mom emerge.

"It's just harder than I thought it would be," she says through difficult breaths. "We've got a long way to go, and I don't know what's going to happen. I want to believe that things will only get better, but I just don't know Chris, I just don't know."

"Mom, I love you, and we are in this together. I'll be home in a few days and we'll talk more, but just know that I really think things are going to be all right. I believe him this time, Mom, I think he is serious about turning things around and putting our family back together."

More tears and difficult breaths on the other end of the phone, "I know honey, don't you worry, you just focus on your classes and finish up strong.... I love you," those three words seem to provoke a steady cry, but still muffled so that dad won't hear from the other room.

"I love you too mom, we'll get through this. I'll see you soon."

"Bye honey."

"Bye mom."

Although I should be celebrating the end of my first semester of college, I don't feel like celebrating. I feel tired. The past year has taken a bigger toll on me than I had realized or imagined, and thank god I didn't know what I would experience in just a couple of days.

I don't know why, but I've always been one for the sentimental. Within my being there exists this desire to pull out every emotion of a given situation to feel it for all its worth. The summer before my senior year in high school is no exception. I'm realizing that one chapter of my life is beginning to wane, and in one year I will be a college student. Life, even with all of the changes and pressures, is very good in this moment. But some emotions don't last as long as I'd like.

It is such an ominous conversation. It is late June and I am in Nashville for the week. Mom's voice over the phone sounds almost too calm, as if she is trying to hide something by using a cloak of tranquility. She said that her and dad were going to pick me up together when I got back into town. Such a strange detail. I know something is brewing, but for the life of me I can't guess what it is. It couldn't be an emergency or she would tell me over the phone, but it is serious enough that she gave me some sense of preparation.

I roll back into town and there they are. In separate cars? I unload my stuff and exchange the usual greetings. We drive the half hour back to our house, I in my mom's car and dad following close behind. My attempts at questioning the situation meet an abrupt stop when my mom continually responds, "We'll talk when we get home."

As we pull into the driveway my questions and fears have become the menacing monster that hides under a kid's bed at night ready to feast on the child when they are least expecting. I, in my seventeen year old athletic body, have begun the transformation to that scared child again. We walk into the house and I see my Uncle Kevin. His presence is both reassuring and frightening; reassuring because he is one of my favorite people in the world, frightening because the seriousness of the situation must be very high to require his tangible presence. We all sit down in the family room.

"Son," a word from Dad's mouth that is both a reassurance of my identity and a reason to grasp the couch tighter, "Mom and I have talked quite a bit, and we have come to the decision that things are a little rough right now. I've decided to move out for the time being until we can get things under control."

"Please understand that this has nothing to do with you or your brother," I'm old enough to understand what Mom is saying, but she doesn't realize that nothing in that statement gives me comfort. "We don't know what is going to happen in the future, we just feel that this is best for right now." They reassure me that Dean, my older brother, has been brought up to speed with the situation given that he is spending the summer in Colorado at a camp for musicians.

My metamorphosis into that scared little boy is complete. I have started at linebacker on my high school football team for two years, I can bench press 300 pounds, I have played against some of the best high school athletes in the state of Indiana, in the eyes of people all around me I am very tough. But now I am a little boy who only wants to crawl on his Mommy's lap and bury his face in his teddy bear. Family has always been the constant in life. No matter what difficulties I have experienced in the past seventeen years, family hasn't changed. When I got cut from the seventh grade basketball team, my family hugged me and restored my self-confidence. When I wore the Guess overalls with a red tag in sixth grade (no one told me that the boy's overalls had a green tag!) it was my family that encouraged me to go to school the next day with my head held high. When we put Caesar, our pure-blooded chow chow, to sleep in the fourth grade, it was my family who laid in bed with me as I cried and grieved my first experience with death. Family never failed ... until now.

The days ahead accelerate my emotional decent. Mom continues to share more details of the separation with me: there are the questionable receipts that she had found, there was Dad's dodging of questions when she asked, and then there was the bank account that she learned had been opened without her consent. Troubling realities with enough force to derail a seventeen year old boy's faith in everything he thought secure.

Weeks passed, and more uncensored truth emerges. When all the pieces are put together there is only one picture, only one truth: dad has chosen someone else over us. I choose not to believe it, that somehow there was another explanation. So, I take it upon myself to investigate. My chasing after the truth ends in a parking lot with a fierce blow to my gut, the car I saw last night parked in front of dad's apartment is the car of the woman we suspected. I get out of my car and walk along the river, because if I don't I may regret my next decision.

The next year was the best and worst year of my life all at the same time. We won our third straight football state championship, defeating a team that was supposed to obliterate us. I was named All-State and invited to play in the state's all-star game. Early in the school year I began dating a girl I was really into. We had so much in common, but more importantly, being with her just felt right. My friend Ryan and I stole street signs, attempted to break into the pool and jump off the rafters, and even put a hole in one of my parent's tires because we did too many doughnuts in a neighborhood cul-de-sac. The year was filled with moments of ecstasy. Moments where I felt like life couldn't get any better.

But all the while there was this haze looming over my head. It was a suffocating haze that threatened my very existence every moment of every day. Every time I accomplished something exciting, it was there. Every test that came back with an A only made me half-smile, every test that came back with a D taunted me with the reality that studying at home was hard because of the reality of my broken family. At senior night I was reminded that even though Mom and Dad were there together, they really weren't. All of these moments lived together inside of me in a painful cocktail that I was forced to drink every day.

In the midst of this reality, football was my drug of choice. Maybe it was the violent nature of the game that allowed my pent up anger to flow out, or maybe it was just simply being at practice, physically away from all that reminded me of my broken family, but I was certainly addicted. Everyone around me fed my addiction too. They told me how good I was. They interviewed me for the newspaper. They made me a captain.

Like a heroin addict I was never satisfied. I was always looking for the next hit, always trying to find a way to garner more praise for my athletic ability.

My efforts did not go in vain. My senior season started out well and I continued to soak within the glory of football success. There was quite a bit of pressure on those of us who were seniors because the previous two seasons our high school had won the Indiana class 5A state championship, and this senior class had a lot of promise. We began the first couple of games by living up to our pre-season hype. When I was on the football field the pain of my parents separation, my dad's lies, my mom's uncontrollable tears, even the deep sadness within my own soul seemed to evaporate, at least until I got back into my car to head home. Despite how elusive those moments of escape were, at least I had them.

I was especially excited about the homecoming game. The team we were playing had a great running back, and my defensive teammates and I were excited about the challenge of shutting him down. It was a crisp October evening, the kind that hinted at fall but was still warm enough for short sleeves. As the first quarter progressed, I found myself having the best game of my high school career. I had two interceptions in the first ten minutes of the game, one which I returned for a touchdown. I clearly remember striding into the end zone after that interception and feeling on top of the world. I didn't even really celebrate when I scored. I just turned towards the home stands and trotted slowly back to our sideline. A sense of pride filled my being, like when you climb your first tree or tie your shoe for the first time and your parents celebrate like you just saved the world. I knew in that moment that mom and dad were in the stands and that I had just given them a reason to be proud of me. It felt good.

On the ensuing kickoff, I ran down the field with more energy than when I started the game. I tackled the ball carrier and we fell to the ground, and right away I knew that something wasn't right. The last time I had laid on the field with an injury was in fifth grade when I got the wind knocked out of me, and seven years later I was just as scared. My coaches helped me off the field as I limped the best I could. My season of glory, my drug of choice, came to a sudden stop. Now, like the rest of my life, my left leg was broken.

I have never been a drug addict. I have never been to rehab. But I think I understand the feeling of numbing your pain for so long and then having that numbing agent taken away all at once.

"Hi, Chris, I'm sorry to interrupt your dinner," Mom was referring to my weekly meal with Lee and Laura. As spring crept closer this husband and wife, who were too old to be a brother and sister but too young to be surrogate parents, invited me to come eat with them at least one night a week. It was a time I dearly looked forward to as they made it very clear that they were committed to walking through this dark valley alongside of me. Throw in Laura's cooking abilities and it didn't take much to convince me.

"It's o.k., Mom, what's up?" A simple question, but I'm not sure if I want to hear the answer.

"Well, I went over to see Dad tonight. I just wanted to see if he needed anything," and why wouldn't she want to see him, he still is her husband. Since Dad moved out last week he is staying temporarily in our motor home at a local campground until he finds a place. This pattern of him moving in and out of our home has been quite draining over the past few months. "When I got there I knocked on the door, and when he opened it *she* was there with him." My hands start to shake ever so slightly as the rage begins to spread throughout my body.

Silence.

How do I possibly respond to the reality that my mom just saw my dad alone with this woman? I am seventeen years old, what words of comfort or advice could I possibly give to my mom?

Mom's tears override my desire to cry. Instead of expressing my hurt and pain I decide that I must be "the man of the house." So, I silently gain my composure and respond, "Mom, I'll be home in twenty minutes, have the keys to the motor home ready for me when I get there."

After words of assurance and love from Lee and Laura, I get in my car to do the one thing in life I never imagined I would have to do, confront my dad in the presence of the woman with whom he is having an affair.

The car ride home is agonizing. My soul is in pieces, but I am so focused on the task at hand that I have this energy pulsating through my veins. It is the same feeling I had in sixth grade right before I got in a fight because someone made fun of my mom, except this time the person I'm going to fight is my dad.

I pull in my driveway and stride intensely into my house. Looking at my mom in this state breaks my heart even more, so I try to keep my interaction with her to a minimum. I have a job to do. I get the keys from her, give her a quick hug and kiss, and get back into my car.

The campground is less than three miles from my house, but in that short drive my mind has already thought through a thousand different scenarios. I pull into the campground and see our motor home. Am I really going to go through with this knee-jerk reaction of an idea? Is this really the best thing to do right now? Before I can answer those questions I am out of my car and walking up to the door.

I put the key in the lock and unlock the door, realizing that now I can't turn back. The door swings open and I enter, shutting the door behind me with great force. I wanted the element of surprise in this situation, and the look on Dad's face when he comes to the front room tells me that I succeeded. I look at him closely and I see anger, sadness, hurt, embarrassment.

"What are you doing here?" he asks.

"I talked with Mom, and I think the question is what are you doing here? This is wrong and you know it," I assert with ferociousness in my voice.

My father has always symbolized strength and leadership. He is the guy, in the words of Tommy Boy, who could sell a ketchup popsicle to a woman wearing white gloves, but right now the roles are reversed and I feel the immense weight of the power I possess in this moment.

"I'm sorry . . . we can talk another time, Chris."

"No, we can talk now." I am aware that although this woman has chosen not to emerge from the back room she can hear the conversation loud and clear. I begin to yell, "You chose her over us. You chose her over me, Dad. How does that make you feel? You are missing my life because of her. Is that what you want?"

"Chris . . ."

I intentionally interrupt, "If this is the choice you are going to make then so be it, I can't make decisions for you. But as for me and Mom, we are going to make our own choices. Make your choice, Dad. Because Mom and I have made ours."

I turn my back on my dad, something I've never done, and storm out of the motor home. As I walk back to my car I can feel my heartbeat in my chest and hands. I just confronted my dad in a way I never have before, and it felt like the right thing to do. In some sense I feel proud that I did it, I stood up for what was right and didn't back down.

But if I did the right thing, then why I am I crying uncontrollably as I pull out of the campground?

The next months pass in a blur. Sure, there are moments to remember: my senior prom, skipping school to go to the beach, the last day of high school, graduation, etc. But blended into every one of those moments are moments of despair, depression, confusion and resentment. Given a choice between the two, I'll take the blur every time.

That summer I was hired by the Boys and Girls Club to work with the kids that attended the summer program. It was the perfect job for two reasons. First, I have always been fond of children. There is an innocence, a purity within children that reminds me of the goodness of humanity, and working with children was exactly what my soul needed. Second, I was able to hook my girlfriend up with a job there as well, so that was just icing on the cake.

These children were different. Many of them came from completely different socioeconomic realities than I did, and it seemed that they had lived through more difficult situations in their short lives than I had experienced in mine. Their eyes told it all. Some boys were wild and out of control, giving in to that primal male instinct of impressing people with their physical prowess, but if you earned the privilege of looking into their eyes for longer than five seconds then you no longer saw a misbehaving kid. Some girls, as young as 6 or 7, communicated with the sassiness of a teenager, but when you colored a picture with them or jumped rope with them you saw in their eyes the simple desire to be accepted. Their eyes told it all.

Mark was a boy unlike the rest. Some of his "other-ness" came from the fact that he was one of the youngest boys there, but there was something more. Despite being five years old, he also wore thick glasses, wasn't very good at sports, and tended to be a little mean. Nonetheless, I liked him, and whether it was the savior complex in me or not I took it upon myself to help him feel accepted and cared for when he came to the club.

Getting his attention was an elusive task in and of itself. Pinning his shadow to the ground may have been easier than getting him to engage something for more then thirty seconds. After numerous failed attempts I did find the one thing that stimulated him to the point where he would at least stay put for a couple of minutes, art. It could be a craft or a decoration project or even just coloring. It quickly became our thing and I prided myself in the fact that Mark would only do these creative ventures with me and no other staff member. Mark and I were good for each other, I found a way to engage him that he enjoyed, and being with him provided me with just enough distraction that I temporarily forgot the brokenness of my home life. I had a sense that it was a much needed deep breath for both of us.

It was difficult at the end of summer trying to break the news to Mark that our time together was almost up. Stories had circulated among the staff about these children, and hearing pieces of Mark's story made me realize even more that the Boys and Girls Club provided both of us with an escape from reality. It saddened me to think that in a couple of months, maybe even a couple of weeks, Mark would forget me and be caught back up into the whirlwind that was his young life. There were lots of hugs between us during that last week, and although I may have made an unhealthy choice by continuing to pursue our relationship throughout the summer knowing that it would end abruptly in a couple of months, I didn't regret it. On one of my last days Mark walked over to me more reserved then I had ever seen him, and I asked him what was up.

"I made dis for you, Kis. For ya ta keep," he exclaimed as he held out an original piece of art he had created depicting the two of us holding hands.

"Mark, this is very special to me, thank you." Although I imagined that he had no intellectual way of comprehending the complete beauty of what he had just done for me and how it affected me, something inside told me that he knew the sacredness of the moment. And so did I. I hugged him and then turned around and wiped the tears from my eyes.

The last few weeks of summer presented me with the reality that to go to college in Ohio meant that I had to leave Mom back in Indiana. That became a very uncomfortable feeling. Although I was just her child, my role, for better or worse over the past year, took on dimensions of a protector. I felt entrusted with a responsibility that I never should have been entrusted with, but I welcomed nonetheless. Somebody had to take care of my mom, and I was the only option while my older brother was away at college. I was the one mom turned to for comfort. I was the one who wiped her tears day after day after day. I remember one day being excused from school because Mom called in requesting me to come home. She had just exposed another one of Dad's lies and she was so sad that she just didn't want to be alone. This type of situation became more and more common. How could I possibly leave her in this state? Living two and a half hours away from her while I was in college was a troubling reality that was quickly approaching.

So exactly when does "manhood," or for that matter "womanhood," begin? At what point do we say goodbye to childhood and enter into adulthood? Is there a magical moment where . . . poof . . . now I'm all grown up? Is there an exact moment, or is it a process that is gradual and less definitive?

I remember when I was a child looking around at all of the adults in my life and at some point I thought, "They are just so . . . different than me." There was such an observable separation between my way of living and thinking and theirs that I imagined entrance into adulthood must come later in life. Of course there must be a moment, at some certain age, that I begin to look like them, talk like them, and think like them. I didn't know when, but I knew it had to happen. Some parts of that "becoming and adult" I looked forward to, others I loathed.

As I learned more about the world I lived in I found out that there are cultures everywhere that do actually have moments where they welcome children into adulthood. In seventh grade I went to my friend Todd's bar mitzvah. Forgetting the fact that much of that Jewish celebration was so foreign to me, I remember hearing the phrase, "Today we welcome Todd into adulthood." What? How come no one welcomed me into adulthood? Todd and I were the same age?

I recently lived in an area where a large portion of our population was Hispanic. Many of my friends and acquaintances were originally from Mexico but found themselves living in this American city. Within the Hispanic community there is a celebration for young women who are turning fifteen called a Quinceañera. It consists of a big party where you welcome a young lady into adulthood. All I got for my fifteenth birthday was a stereo.

I once had a friend who spent a lot of time in the Dakotas with the Native American Lakota tribe. There is a coming of age ritual that has been practiced in the history of this people for many years called "The Vision Quest." It is a complicated ritual with the goal of allowing a young person between the ages of ten and thirteen to experience solitude so as to hear from the Great Spirit regarding their direction in life.

These are just three examples of cultures that seek to consciously welcome children into adulthood at a certain point in time. I imagine that not only is there a change within the way the community views the young person after the ceremony, but there must also be a very real change that occurs within the psyche of the "new" adult. If everyone around me recognizes me as an adult, then maybe I will begin to think of myself that way. Like a computer, the input will equal the output. Maybe I will start to think of the world and my place in it outside of the self-centeredness that defined my childhood.

Our society is different though. We have a word that we throw around that gives young people the justification they need to remain childlike, sometimes long into their 20's or 30's. It is the term adolescence. An adolescent is someone who is not a child but not yet an adult. It is a time where irresponsibility is assumed and welcomed; I have even heard the phrase, "Oh, that's just what adolescents do." This phrase seeks to excuse unbelievably destructive behavior because these young people are not yet expected to act with maturity and responsibility. There is an entire market created within our society for this period. There are magazines, television shows, movies, beauty products, etc. that seek to promote this age of irresponsibility. Is this a good alternative?

As I reflect on this reality a thought hits me, maybe there is a coming of age ceremony within our society that a majority of young people go through. It isn't always planned, but it has similar effects upon the young adult as those other cultural coming of age ceremonies. It changes the participant's worldview. It signifies, at least in some way, the end of childhood. It often shifts the focus of the child so intensely that they begin to interpret the world through different eyes. And in some of these ceremonies the children are even expected to make very difficult, life altering decisions. The ceremony I refer to is the ceremony of divorce, and many of my friends went through this coming-of-age ceremony.

Many children that experience the devastating reality of broken families understand, in one way or another, that the care-free days of childhood are over. Try telling a seven year old that they have to be at two different places for Christmas. Observe, as I recently did, the demeanor of a fourteen year old boy who has to leave his mom behind and fly on an airplane so that he can spend Thanksgiving with his dad. Go ahead and answer the questions of a ten year old who asks why she can't hang out with her friends every other weekend because she will be out of town.

I know for me that the falling apart of my family changed me in ways I didn't expect, and I was seventeen years old. All of a sudden, whatever innocence was left in my being flew out the window and was replaced by the stark, hurtful reality of broken relationships. Rainbows were all of a sudden less magical, birthdays less special, and holidays less refreshing. Through the words of many around me and the thoughts in my own head, now was the time I became a "man."

My first semester of college began well. I was roommates with a friend of mine from my high school, Anthony, and we, along with his twin brother Aaron, played on our university's football team. It was nice not having to go through the awkward pseudo-friendship period that you go through with a complete stranger. Instead, I enjoyed the familiarity that came with sleeping in the same room with somebody I already trusted and shared a friendship.

Meeting people is a big part of what the college experience entails, and I've never been an introvert, so engaging new people came pretty easily. Lunch is an especially opportune time to meet new people, which for guys is code for "sit next to the most attractive member of the opposite sex with the hopes of walking away with a phone number." Given the reality that I was already in a very enjoyable relationship with my girlfriend from high school, I didn't enter into mealtime with the same goal as the rest of my football teammates. I just wanted to make new friends.

One day, not long after the term began, I made the uneventful walk across campus to the cafeteria for lunch. My roommate had other responsibilities that day, so as far as I was concerned I was dining alone. I knew I could probably find some of my teammates to eat with, but something about that thought didn't excite me very much. Collegiate football players and food don't always create the most pleasant dining experience.

To my surprise much of the cafeteria was empty by the time I arrived. A few students still lingered either engrossed in one on one conversation or with their noses buried within books, thick books. I assumed that I could probably get by with a quiet, serene lunch this day, and something about that thought refreshed me. Meandering my way through the different cuisines, I settled on a sandwich and its typical sides. I admit I was disappointed, but I had yet to lower my expectations regarding the college dining experience.

I made my way back into the dining section when I saw someone familiar. His name took a minute to come to me, but what I did remember about this teammate of mine was that he was one of the most obnoxiously vocal guys on our team. He was the guy who was always jawing with somebody about something. If it didn't have to do with football then it was about religion, if it wasn't about religion then it was about classes, if it wasn't about classes, then it was about music, if it wasn't about music, then it was about something else, and sitting with him at lunch didn't seem too intriguing of a proposition. As soon as I came to that conclusion he got vocal, "Hey man what's up, you want to sit here?"

"Sure, thanks man," I replied, all the while hoping he thought I was sincere.

"Your c-dub right?" a name I had inherited because of my initials. "I'm Drew. Your roommate told me that we needed to hook up and talk sometime."

"O.k., so, why did you think he said that?"

"I don't know I guess he thought we had some things in common. What's your story?"

And how exactly was I supposed to respond to that? Does this guy really care about my whole story, or is he just asking out of curiosity? I went with the latter and proceeded to talk mostly about my experiences in football and my girlfriend (yes, unfortunately in that order).

Not two seconds after I finished my monologue Drew asked, "So, are your parents together?"

Wow, this guy doesn't mess around. I tentatively looked up from my meal and responded, "Actually things are pretty rough right now." That was the most I could muster without becoming emotionally attached to the conversation in a way I didn't intend. "What about you?"

"My parents just got divorced, a little over a year ago. I have a little sister too, and it has torn us up on the inside." I was blown away. Here was this overly vocal offensive lineman who on the outside appeared to have the swagger of someone with great confidence, but just confessed to me that on the inside he is hurt and broken . . . just like me. Somewhere in that moment all the stereotypes I had of Drew went out the window and I imagined that the lunch we shared may turn into a friendship that both of us desperately needed. As the meal went on we continued to share our stories gradually progressing deeper and deeper into the painful details of both of our situations. When we eventually got up from the table we both knew that we weren't as alone as we had felt before that meal.

Drew and I continued to seek out our friendship with intentionality. The overly vocal-ness that had bothered me before, all of a sudden became a reassuring sound of his presence in the midst of my hurt. As weeks went on we decided that we wanted to dive further into our pain. We read a story together of a man who lost everything: his children, possessions, health. Then, three of his friends came to comfort him, and before they said a word they sat with him for seven days. Our hope was that in reading this ancient story we may gain some insight into our own suffering and brokenness. Despite having no real idea of how to read ancient stories, our little experiment benefited us in some real ways. We came to the conclusion that sometimes the best response to someone's suffering is simply just being with them, and letting go of the pressure to fabricate something profound to say. Perhaps just being present was enough.

Only a couple of weeks went by before we had the chance to test our new hypothesis. There was this teammate of ours named Russ that Drew and I had both gotten to know. Now Russ was only about an inch taller than me, but it was the sixty extra pounds of solid muscle surrounding his frame that set he and I apart. Russ was very likeable, one of those guys that saw life through very simple lenses. He told you what he felt and why without feeling any need to justify feeling that way, and something about that was very endearing. Russ soon became another friend Drew and I were around a lot. Russ got a call on a Friday, the day before one of our games, that his dad had experienced a massive heart attack at his home, and he didn't make it. The news affected me in many ways, but Russ's well being was my greatest concern. Drew and I didn't know what to do, other than to express to him by our presence that we were with him through his suffering. The funeral came and went and Drew and I continued to try to be the best friends we could to our teammate who had just lost his daddy.

It wasn't long after the news of Russ's dad that my thoughts went to my dad. Some thoughts, when unleashed in your mind, find a way of escaping the mind and taking up residence in your heart and soul. What if my dad died suddenly? How could I ever live in the reality that my dad, who had been my hero for my entire life, and I had a relationship that was ... broken? I was angry at my dad, but he was still my dad. How could I live with that anger if something happened to him? Would I feel guilt the rest of my life for feeling angry? These thoughts along with many others were not my friends.

Although my dad and I had spoken sporadically throughout the term, and he had come to all of my home games (even though I wasn't playing), I certainly didn't expect his phone call when it came in late October.

"Hi Chris."

"Hey Dad."

"I was wondering if I could come visit you in a weekend or two? I have a lot I want to share with you, and I think we could use some fun together."

If hope begins as a spark, then nothing less than an explosion happened in me at that moment. The past year had taught me numerous lessons on the experience of failed hopes and expectations, but something in his voice made me hope again.

"Yeah, that sounds good to me. When are you thinking about coming?"

"Probably a week or two, but I'll let you know. Chris, I love you and I miss you."

"I love you too Dad."

I would be lying to say that I wasn't tired of the emotional roller coaster of the past year, but I couldn't help but think that Dad's visit would be the much needed moment of reconciliation between the two of us. I missed my daddy.

Dad came to visit on a blustery November weekend. The anxiety that resided in me the days leading up to his visit were equal to the anxiety of the finals that loomed in the near future. It was a strange feeling being anxious about seeing my dad, but this anxiety was a welcomed emotion in light of the others I had felt over the past year. He arrived and like a puppy left at home too long I flew to the door to greet him. We hugged ... and it felt like Dad again.

We didn't have any big plans. Our intention was just to spend the day together: lunch, maybe a movie and probably a trip to stock me up with some snacks for the last couple of weeks until Christmas break.

The day was everything I had hoped. While we ate lunch at Bob Evans (Dad's choice 9 times out of 10) he shared with me his thoughts. He had reached a low point a couple of months ago and decided that he didn't have to live life this way. That began a very slow but very intentional pattern of communication with Mom. He knew he had lost her trust, and he didn't pretend that she owed it to him right away. But they kept talking. He then expressed to me that he had asked mom about the possibility of moving back into our house once and for all. No more lies, no more gimmicks. He was ready to choose his family. For the first time in all of the pain of the past year I felt like I could see some light at the end of the hell I was walking through. Could this really be possible? Could our family really be restored?

After lunch we went to a movie, but my mind was far from the movie. I wondered what it would feel like to go through a day without worrying about the emotional state of one or both of my parents. Dad and I laughed a lot through that movie, but I think for both of us it wasn't just the movie that gave us reason to laugh.

Our time together was drawing to a close, but there was still one more event that weighed heavy on my mind. In preparation for this visit I had crafted a letter to Dad. It was a letter with one intention: begin the healing process between us. However, in the three page letter I was honest about the depth of pain I experienced over the past year, and I was nervous about how Dad would take it. We went back to my dorm room and he sat on my bed. His face was different in that moment; he didn't look defensive. I handed him the letter, and when his wise, rough hands took it I held my breath. Never before had I spoken to my father like I did in that letter, and now it was in his hands and I couldn't turn back.

I watched as his eyes scanned each line slowly. Dad was a fast reader, everyone knew that, so his choice to read through my letter slowly both scared me and encouraged me. The couple minutes it took to read the letter was hours as far as my brain was concerned. Finally, he had read the last word and slowly lowered the letter. I continued to hold my breath as I tentatively awaited his reaction.

"That is a beautiful letter my son. Thank you."

When I began to exhale we were already hugging . . . and crying. It was the kind of tears that felt good to stream down your face. Tears that carried with them so many hurtful emotions but were now literally and symbolically falling away.

"You're welcome Dad. I love you."

Preparing for finals became a much easier task after our reconciliatory reunion. As a matter of fact a few weeks later we celebrated Thanksgiving together as a family. None of us pretended that the road ahead would be trite and simple, but that didn't stop us from celebrating. That holiday was the first time in over a year that I was able to be home without the pressure of holding everything together. It was a refreshing and welcomed change.

The two weeks left of college after Thanksgiving break pretty much equate to the day before summer vacation in an elementary school. Everyone is stir crazy because the term is almost done and a much deserved break is ahead. These concluding weeks were even more energizing for me given the renewed hope in the restoration of my family. After all, I would be going home to my *family*, and that is much more than I expected at the beginning of the term.

The most settling feeling in the midst of this whole situation was knowing that Mom wasn't going to continue to suffer. If Dad is serious, then her days of excruciating despair were behind her. That gave me unspeakable solace.

However, when I talk to Mom on the phone I begin to worry. She often cries at some point in the conversation and expresses to me the reality that although Dad may have good intentions, the long road ahead isn't going to be easy. This is something I realize, but it seems as if Mom isn't telling me the whole story. Sometimes when we are talking on the phone she sneaks to another room so that Dad won't hear her crying. This worries me, both her crying and her sneaking. I begin to get a disturbing feeling deep in my gut, but I fight it because I am tired of disturbing feelings. As a matter of fact, I begin to realize just how tired I am.

The term ends well. I aced my finals and started my collegiate experience exactly how I wanted to academically. Over a day and a half I organize my things and try to pack as much as I can into my 2-door Ford Escort. It's trickier than it seems, but the thought of going home and sleeping in my own bed excites me and makes the packing process that much easier. I say goodbye to my new friends, exchange addresses and a few CD's and I am on my way home!

I arrive home on a Tuesday, ten days before Christmas. This season is one that my entire family looks forward to, and the aura of my house expresses that excitement. The banister which leads upstairs is covered with fake evergreen, rhythmically spiraled all the way up; there are plush stuffed creatures attached to the railing that greet you every time you walk in the foyer: an elf, two reindeer, a nutcracker soldier, two snowmen and Santa himself. The outside of our house glows with the beam of hundreds of tiny light bulbs carefully woven into the landscape. Mom has begun the traditional, yet lengthy, process of baking more desserts then we could ever eat: sugar cookies with detailed icing, gingerbread men, and orange cookies to name the favorites. From the outside, all seems well.

Wednesday is my first official day of Christmas break. I wake up lazily and eventually get dressed. The scheduled visit with my girlfriend, Christi, is at the top of my to-do list for the day. I am going to go see her briefly this morning and then she is going to come hang out at our house later that evening. Our relationship, which has grown since we began dating our senior year in high school, is very meaningful to me, and I am convinced that the feeling is reciprocal.

After a short visit with her I head back home, feeling very satisfied with life. Not that life is perfect, but it certainly is good. When I get home Mom is preparing her dough and getting all the items in order for the baking process. Dad has gone to work and his absence presents an opportunity that I am reluctant to take but feel I must.

"So, Mom, how are you and Dad? Honestly."

Maybe it was the adverb I stuck in at the end of my question, but something gave her pause, and in my recollection pauses equal trouble. She keeps working but begins to tell me story after story of the past few weeks. Her worst fear is that Dad's affair is not done. She has hints and clues that point in that horrific direction, but she can't be sure. Who can blame her? How can she be sure of anything at this point?

As I listen to her stories and the evidence she is mounting in her head, I realize that what I see before me is a woman who is exhausted from the fight. These doubts, fears, wounds, facades of happiness have all worn her down so so much. I have seen this exhaustion before. Much of my senior year of high school it was evident. It's just harder to see now. I was so confident that we were making strides as a family and that Dad had turned things around for real, but now Mom isn't sure. I recognize that her mind is processing all this information through filters of hurt and pain so I try to balance her fears with my own thoughts of hope, but her tears are stronger than my hopes. I find myself afraid again. I hug Mom and try to reassure her that things will be o.k. this time. She goes along with my weak logic, but part of me knows she doesn't really believe it.

Later that evening Christi comes over and we spend time watching a movie and helping Mom ice cookies. Dad is home sitting in his recliner. In those moments, all seems so normal, so right. It's as if my brain chooses when I will remember the reality of the situation, and tonight is not one of those nights. Tonight is a good night! I say goodnight to Christi, and not long after, I say goodnight to my parents. That feels good, to be able to say goodnight to both of them in the same house once again. Maybe there is hope.

I am startled awake Thursday morning and not completely coherent. What time is it? 6:00a.m. I rub my eyes and realize that I was awoken by my parents' voices down the hall. They are in their room fighting. The part of me that has played protector to my mother over the past year and half gets out of bed. I walk softly down the hall so I can listen by their door. My parents have never been violent with each other, so that wasn't my concern. I simply wanted to make sure that I didn't need to step into the midst of the fight to calm things down.

After only a few minutes their voices lower and it seems as if the situation has dissolved. I am grateful I didn't have to enter their fight. I stumble back to bed and decide to call Christi before going back to sleep. Her voice calms me and soothes me and I apologize for waking her. Now I can get back to sleep. Before I drift off again I remember that I set my alarm for 7:00 a.m. so I could get up and work out. I decide to work out later in the day and grant myself a morning of sleeping in.

The alarm goes off at 9:00 a.m. I have a meeting this morning with a teacher from my high school. During my first semester of college I found myself intrigued by the field of psychology and I have a few questions for this teacher regarding a career in that field. As I go about my morning routine I notice that my house is quiet. It is a much different reality then the dorm life I've been living in for the past few months.

When I am all ready to go I grab some paper for notes, a CD and my keys. I say goodbye to my brother who is sitting in the family room and open the door to my garage. It is colder than I expected. From the doorway I notice that both of my parents cars are here. Odd.

I walk out of the garage to a sight I don't comprehend right away. My parents are lying down in the grass next to the driveway. All of a sudden I wake up to the situation, everything I am carrying falls to the ground. I run to them and shake my mom. I touch my dad. There is a gun by my Mom's hand. My parents are dead.

2

Irrevocable Loss

> *"A human's suffering is similar to the behavior of gas.*
> *If a certain quantity of gas is pumped into an empty chamber,*
> *it will fill the chamber completely and evenly,*
> *no matter how big the chamber.*
> *Thus suffering completely fills the human soul and conscious mind,*
> *no matter whether the suffering is great or little."*
>
> —Viktor Frankl

I CAN READ ABOUT stories of unexplainable grief; I can watch movies that depict great loss and suffering, some of them even based on true events; I can watch the news night after night and hear their depressing monologues that describe the latest and worst tragedy; but until I live through the fierce reality of my own loss, it is just another story. I may be moved by the stories I see and hear and read. They may even shape me in how I understand the world and my place in it, but until it was my parents that died, until it was my Great Sadness,[1] empathy was elusive.

Not long after coming out of the garage that Thursday morning, I became aware that there are stories of suffering all around me. My eyes were opened to the sufferers that I would not have noticed before. Yes, my suffering may be unique but it is still connected to the suffering of others. I have seen pictures of Holocaust survivors holding hands with war veterans. I have seen images of victims from 9/11 crying with the victims of bombings in Iraq. I continue to be inspired at the sight of Bishop Desmond Tutu and the Dalai Lama hugging each other and smiling together as they remember their shared, but unique, struggle for

---

1. A simple but moving phrase from William P. Young, *The Shack*, 16.

human dignity and worth. All of these people have different stories of suffering, but even in their differences, suffering unites them.

Human beings have experienced suffering throughout every step of their history. Some of the most ancient stories we have discovered communicate the axiom that to be human, is to suffer. The earliest pieces of Western literature to emerge in history are Homer's dual works, *The Iliad* and *The Odyssey*. These stories are dated sometime around 700 BCE, and their plots center around the themes of war, loss, love, desire, and death, all themes deeply connected to human suffering. As a matter of fact the plot of *The Odyssey* begins with Odysseus's son, Telemachus, "dreaming of how his noble father might come back from out of the blue."[2] It is Telemachus' longing to see his absent father, and his subsequent suffering, that moves the plot forward.

There is this ancient Mesopotamian story written in the Akkadian language called *Enuma Elish* that tells of the creation of the world. In this story the gods are territorial, angry, and eventually end up creating human beings out of the carcass of a slain god. After Marduk, the chief god, creates human beings he explains the purpose of the human race, "[Humans] shall be charged with the service of the gods that they [the gods] might be at ease!"[3] In *Enuma Elish* the goal for the gods is that they could inflict the humans with all of the work that has to be done so that they may rest. Even in spite of the fact that the humans suffer greatly because of the gods, the gods simply do not care.

I watched a movie recently, based on a true story, where a mother went to work one day and when she returned from work her young son was missing. The rest of the plot of the movie was driven forward by this mother's relentless pursuit of her lost son. Her suffering became the central theme that drove the plot forward.

Whether they are literally thousands of years old or only a couple of weeks old, humans have always been drawn to stories that tell of suffering. Why is this? Perhaps the answer to that question lies in the reality that stories of suffering empower humans to engage their own personal suffering. Maybe it simply reminds us that we are not alone in our suffering, that there are other people in the world, even if they lived at a different time, who have walked down paths just as dark and lonely and scary as ours.

2. Homer, *The Odyssey*, 28.
3. Speiser, *The Creation Epic*, 36.

Some of these stories are primarily meant for entertainment, like the movie I watched, but some of them actually give us insight into how human beings have worked through their suffering at different times and different places. If we learn to listen to these stories then we quickly become aware that there is a timeless universality to the human experience. No matter how "advanced" we think we are, no matter how different we think we are, we are all human. Despite our intellectual, socio-economic, cultural, and temporal differences, when we hear stories of joy and loss we can empathize. For example, there is this ancient story, at least 2,500 years old, of a man named Jacob who steals something from his brother and lies to his father. So Jacob runs away. He actually thinks that he can outrun his problems.[4] One of my favorite bands has this song where the chorus speaks of how much easier it is to run from our problems and numb our pain instead of facing it head on.[5] How is it that an ancient story from thousands of years ago about a man running from his problems sounds a lot like a song written by a band in 2003? Maybe being human in the twenty-first century CE is not all that different from being human in the sixth century BCE.

This is why I want to introduce you to some friends of mine, the Judeans of the seventh–sixth century BCE. Their story is different than ours, but at the same time it is very similar. Their suffering has been told many times, and if we seek to listen closely to their voices, then maybe, just maybe, we can learn more about ourselves and more about our suffering.

Why should we care about a group of people so different from us whose story is a couple millennia old? What could they possibly offer us, especially in regards to our suffering? Aren't we so much more advanced than they were? Yes, we are very different and more technologically advanced, but maybe if we look closely at what defined this group of people we will see that our differences are trivial in light of our similarities.

Like us, the people of Judah had a history that defined and shaped how they interacted with the world. They believed certain things were good and beautiful and worth living for. They believed some ways of living were destructive and harmful. They also defined their place within

---

4. Genesis 27–28.
5. Linkin Park, *Easier to Run*.

the world by the stories that had been passed down to them by their grandparents and their grandparents grandparents and on and on.

The story that defined this group of people begins with a god who speaks and acts very differently from the gods of the other cultures around them.[6] This god creates, and then, like a toddler who has just drawn a bunch of pictures, constantly gives away what is created so other creatures can enjoy it. This god begins by creating light, and then separating light from darkness. A bit later in the story God gives this job of separating light from darkness to two great lights. Then, God creates sky and oceans, but eventually God gives the sky and oceans to the birds and sea creatures. Next, God creates dry ground, and then, like the other pieces of creation, God gives it away to all kinds of animals that walk on the ground. This god can't stop giving things away. This god doesn't have control issues.[7]

The crown jewels of creation, according to this story, are the human beings. These human beings are so important that they are the only piece of creation that is created in the "image" of this god; male and female created in this god's image. God then tells the first humans to work with the creation and take care of it, presumably the way that this god would take care of it. So, to be a Judean living in the sixth century BCE meant, at the most basic level, that the god of all creation has invited you to join in taking care of the world.

But the story goes south from there. These first humans are tricked into thinking that they are incomplete in some way, so they eat fruit from a tree that was never meant to be eaten. By eating this fruit, so they are told, they can be like God. The problem is that they were already like God, they bore his image. They were complete exactly how they were, but that wasn't enough for them. After they finished eating their fruit salad, they quickly realized that for the first time in history relationships were broken. All of a sudden things were not how God created them to be.

So God responds, because this god is not satisfied with leaving things broken. This god, who eventually wants to be called Yahweh (Yahway),[8] comes to a man named Abram and says,

---

6. The most comprehensive and beneficial comparison between Israel's creation narrative and Mesopotamian creation narratives is arguably Richard Middleton's, *The Liberating Image*.

7. Genesis 1.

8. My choice to attempt to vocalize the tetragrammaton (the four letter name of God in Hebrew) is in no way intended to offend my Jewish friends. It is simply my attempt to faithfully communicate the narrative of the Hebrew Bible/Old Testament in

> Go from your country, your people and your father's household to the land I will show you. I will make you a great nation and I will bless you; I will make your name great and you will be a blessing. I will bless those who bless you, and whoever curses you I will curse; and all peoples on earth will be blessed through you.[9]

Did you catch it? This Yahweh has a plan for dealing with the brokenness: invite a group of human beings to show the rest of the world what this god is like. So, through their interaction with the rest of the world this group of people will bring healing, life, restoration, and reconciliation to everyone and everything by living Yahweh's way... at least that is the hope. This group of people is "elected" by Yahweh to be the presence of God in the world. Yahweh does not want to put the brokenness back together all alone, Yahweh wants humans to get in on the fun too. Then, in an act of loving care Yahweh changes Abram's name to Abraham, and his wife Sarai's name to Sarah, completing the adoption process.

The plan, however, takes a turn for the worst when Abraham's descendants find themselves, a handful of generations later, enslaved by the Egyptian empire. The question arises, how can these people be everything Yahweh dreamt they could be while in slavery? The intense language used to describe their situation illuminates the oppression under which they lived, "The children of Israel let out a hopeless sigh because of their slavery, which eventually turned into a desperate scream. Their scream, because of their slavery, went up to God."[10] Slavery is opposed to everything Yahweh desired for creation. So, in response to their slavery scream Yahweh stepped in, and, through a dramatic progression, dethroned the king of Egypt and rescued the people from their slavery. Yahweh then led them through a desert to a mountain where an exchange occurred between Yahweh and the people, reminiscent of a marriage ceremony. This story of rescue from slavery in Egypt becomes a dominant theme of remembrance for this people far into their future. Yahweh's identity becomes centrally located within this story of rescue. To know this story of liberation is to know who Yahweh is.

Following their liberation, the people organize themselves into twelve tribes united together in their commitment to living Yahweh's

---

a way that would make sense to anyone who is unfamiliar with this literature.

9. Genesis 12:1–3.
10. Exodus 2:23, my translation.

way. They eventually realized that if they were going to be a real world superpower, then they needed to stop living a tribal life and have a king rule over them. Apparently they forgot that "world superpower" was not in their job description. Nonetheless, they organized themselves into a kingdom ruled by one man. All was quiet until sometime around the year 920 BCE when the united nation of Israel split into two nations: Israel and Judah.[11] The northern ten tribes were referred to as Israel or Ephraim, and the southern two tribes were referred to as Judah. The city of Jerusalem, which had been the political and religious capital of the united nation, now was in the territory of Judah. So much had gone wrong so quickly.

If we were Judeans living in the sixth century BCE, this is the story that would captivate our imaginations. This is how we would understand the world in which we lived. This would define who we would be. Despite the schism that now divided the united Israel into two nations, we would still bear within our minds the realization that we were Yahweh's answer to a broken world. Yes, that is a lot of pressure, but we would be up for it.

If I said the word "pyramids," I imagine that most of us would immediately think of Egypt, and images of vast, sandy deserts would come to our minds. If I said "Eiffel Tower" many would think of Paris. If I said "The Great wall of _____" a majority would fill in the blank with the word "China." If I said "Declaration of Independence" we could not help but think of the United States.

Every nation, every people group has characteristics that define them. They all have symbols that are important both to their history and to their present circumstances. Most cultures have holidays that recall special moments within their history, moments that have brought them to where they are in the present. Also, every group of people in the world has some type of communal structure. Whether it is a tribal structure, a dictatorship, a republic, etc., without some form of organization, chaos is inevitable.

If you have grown up in the United States then it is not very hard to name the symbols, holidays, and communal structure that define that

---

11. Bright, *History of Israel*, 229.

nation. If you listen closely to all three then you can hear the story of the United States that has made it what it is today.

The same is true of the Judeans. We may not be able to talk to a Judean of the sixth century BCE today, but if we look at their symbols, holidays, and communal structure maybe we can understand this group of people a little better, which will hopefully give us ears to hear their story of suffering.

Of the many symbols that helped to define the Judeans I think the two that best encapsulate their story are the temple and the tassels.

The temple was the central place of worship for Yahweh's people. But it wasn't just a place where a bunch of people came together to sing songs about Yahweh. The temple was the place where the divine and the human intermingled. It was where heaven and earth touched. It was so central to this people that three times every year the entire nation would journey to the temple to celebrate who Yahweh is and what Yahweh had done.[12]

The temple was a building, but it was so much more than a building. It was the one space where you, as a citizen of the nation of Israel, could be reminded of your place in the world. Your place, whose roots stem from a conversation between Yahweh and Abram; a life lived on behalf of others. It was a way of living so countercultural yet so beautifully inviting, that other nations would look at how you lived and be in awe.[13] This was why the temple existed. Life is difficult, and I imagine that the Judeans were a lot like you and me. They sometimes got so focused on themselves or on their narrow view of the world that they needed reminders that there was a whole world out there waiting for someone to embody hope and life. The temple was the rallying point for these revolutionaries of hope.

The second symbol, the tassels, originates in an instruction given to the Israelites in Numbers 15:37-41:[14]

> Yahweh said to Moses, "Speak to the Israelites and say to them: 'Throughout the generations to come you are to make tassels on

---

12. Exodus 23:14-17, Deuteronomy 16:16-17.
13. Deuteronomy 4:5-8.
14. This section of text along with Deuteronomy 6:4-9 and Deuteronomy 11:13-21 form what is, and has been, the central prayer to the heart of the Jewish people. It is referred to as the *Shema* which is the first Hebrew word in Deuteronomy 6:4. *Shema* means to listen, hear, obey.

> the corners of your garments, with a blue cord on each tassel. You will have these tassels to look at and so you will remember all the commands of Yahweh, that you may obey them and not prostitute yourselves by chasing after the lusts of your own hearts and eyes. Then you will remember to obey all my commands and will be consecrated to your God. I am Yahweh your God, who brought you out of Egypt to be your God. I am Yahweh your God."

You see, for an Israelite, the commandments of Yahweh were life giving. When we hear the word "commandment" we either think of 10 religious rules that people hang on their walls,[15] or we think of those who give commands, like drill sergeants. Unfortunately, neither of those images do justice to how the Israelites viewed the commandments of Yahweh. A friend of mine once explained it to me this way: if you break your arm and I give you instructions on how to take care of it, how to cast it, how to wear it in a sling, when to take the cast off, etc., you wouldn't say to me, "You are just trying to control me with your rules," or, "Your laws are so burdensome." No, you would thank me for showing you how to help heal your broken bone.[16] You would be grateful for those instructions.

In the same way Yahweh's people were grateful for his instructions and commandments. They believed that following the commandments of Yahweh actually brought more life, more hope, and more healing everywhere they went. So, these tassels on the corners of their garments were intended to be a tangible reminder of Yahweh's life-giving commandments. It reminded them of their story. It reminded them of all the things Yahweh had done for them, going all the way back to a conversation with Abram. Now we can understand why a couple of threads attached to the corner of their clothes became so much more than just a couple of threads. Those threads became a symbol reminding them of Yahweh's love and care, as expressed in the commandments.

What about holidays? I have walked with groups of people on Martin Luther King Jr. day in cold, wet weather because we understood that to remember Dr. King's story is important. It was just another day, but it was so much more than a day. It recalled a story that many of us do

---

15. Ironically, Exodus 20 and Deuteronomy 5 are not referred to in the Hebrew as "commandments." Rather, they are called Yahweh's words. Thus, "ten words" are a more accurate description and translation than "ten commandments."

16. Absolutely brilliant Drew!

not want to ever forget. What about Judah? What stories did they want to make sure they never forgot?

There were seven festivals in the calendar year that the people of Yahweh were supposed to celebrate, and all of them reenacted a piece of their story as a people. Three of them had extra significance: the Festival of Unleavened Bread, the Festival of Weeks, and the Festival of Tabernacles. It was during these three holidays that, unlike the other holidays, all of Yahweh's people would travel to the temple to celebrate.

The Festival of Unleavened Bread was exactly what it sounds like. The people would come together and for seven days, among other things, eat bread that was made without yeast. It was eating this yeast-less bread that reminded them of a central part of their story as a people. For 430 years Yahweh's people were in slavery in Egypt. But how could slaves fulfill Yahweh's dream of being a blessing to all people? They couldn't. So, Yahweh acted on their behalf and provided the way for them to escape their slavery. The night before they left Egypt Yahweh instructed them to eat bread without yeast, which obviously took less time to make, because when you are trying to escape out of slavery haste takes precedence.

The Festival of Weeks, which was eventually called Pentecost, was a celebration held fifty days after the first harvest of wheat or other grains. Central to this festival is being reminded that it is Yahweh that sends the rain and sun for the crops to grow. There is so much about the growing process that we humans do not control. Farmers may till the ground, remove the weeds, plant the seed, but nothing the farmer does causes the seed to explode with life. The Festival of Weeks was a time to be reminded that at its most elemental level food is a gift.

However, there is also an ancient rabbinic tradition connected to the Festival of Weeks. It says that when Yahweh freed the Israelites from slavery in Egypt it took them fifty days to travel to Mount Sinai. When they arrived at Mount Sinai, Yahweh asked Moses to come up the mountain to receive instructions for the newly freed people. This is considered the marriage ceremony of Yahweh and the Israelites. At this time the people were invited into a certain way of living that was distinct to Yahweh's followers. Within Israel's story this is referred to as the covenant. Thus, the rabbis taught that the Festival of Weeks was also a time to remember the giving and receiving of Yahweh's instructions.[17]

---

17. b. B. Sha. 86b, this refers to the Babylonian Talmud, an ancient Jewish document that contains rabbinic discussion pertaining to Jewish law and practice.

So, along with celebrating how Yahweh provided food from the earth, the Festival of Weeks was also a time to remember the covenant Yahweh made with the people.

The Festival of Tabernacles was a week long party where everybody would live in a temporary shelter for a week, kind of like camping except it took more work to build the shelter. The point of living in the shelters and celebrating for the week was to remember that Yahweh brought them out of slavery in Egypt and while they were traveling away from Egypt they lived in temporary shelters.

We can easily see why these holidays were so important to the Judeans, because they recalled their communal story. I imagine if I was a Judean parent I would be grateful for these perennial celebrations. They would give me the opportunity to have an entire week to stop working, be with my family, and share with my children the significance of the stories that defined us as a people.

Now that we have looked at the symbols and holidays central to the Judeans, what about Judah's communal structure? How did they organize themselves? What was unique about their communal structure?

As we noted above, Yahweh's people organized themselves into tribes not long after leaving Egypt. There were twelve tribes, each with a tribal leader. As time went on they even appointed groups of people to oversee different decisions that needed to be made. It wasn't perfect, but it worked for them. In the midst of this tribal structure there was the understanding that even though different people had different leadership roles, ultimately it was Yahweh who was the head of all. Yahweh was *the* leader of the people, and the people wanted it that way.

This tribal life lasted for some time until, like a pre-teen fit of jealousy, the people demanded a king so that they could be like all the other nations. This hurt Yahweh's feelings, but Yahweh allowed them to have what they wanted.[18] The only catch: Israel's king was supposed to look very different than any other king in the world. This king was supposed to embody Yahweh's values, characteristics, and instructions; he wasn't supposed to accumulate large amounts of wealth. He was not supposed to be manipulative with his power and have many wives. Most importantly, he wasn't supposed to think that he was better than everyone else

---

18. See 1 Samuel 8.

just because he was king. As we can see, this king was supposed to be different.[19]

Now that you have met my friends the Judeans, let's cautiously enter into their story of suffering with our eyes and ears open.[20]

It is fascinating to me how life can lull us into rhythms and patterns and expectations that are easily sustained. Let's be honest, we enjoy the lull. It is not a bad thing, but then one day the lull, the rhythm, the expected gets disrupted by the unexpected. Life is then disorienting, confusing, and ultimately unknown. The lull taught us what to expect in the future, but now it has been replaced with the scary, unpredictable reality of the unknown.

Imagine walking down the streets of Jerusalem on your way to the temple. The warmth of the bright sun soothes you as you turn the corner past another building and see it. It is a massive structure created with so much care and detail that even those who do not worship Yahweh are impressed with its aesthetic quality. For hundreds of years it has been the center of worship for your people, and it gives you a sense of pride to know that this beautiful structure serves as the identifiable symbol of the nation of Judah. Even more than that, though, the temple is the place where Yahweh's presence is most abundant.

Something is different this day, and as you approach the gate you notice the crowd. Crowds aren't that abnormal around the temple, what is out of the ordinary is that this massive crowd is completely silent. All of the crowd's attention is focused sharply on one individual. You pick up your pace to try to make it in time to catch what is so intriguing about what this individual is saying. Unfortunately, as you arrive to the outer edges of the crowd they begin to disperse, and their faces communicate clearly their disgust with whatever was just spoken. Some of them are leaving and some of them are angrily crowding around the man who just spoke. You try to listen to the murmurings of the people as they walk away but you cannot make out anything intelligible. Then, you hear something so offensive that you jerk your head in the direction from

---

19. Deuteronomy 17:14–20.

20. Much of what follows is influenced by Louis Stulman's works: *Jeremiah* and *Order Amid Chaos*.

where it came. The disgust of the crowd now colors your face as you process the two words you just heard: Temple destroyed.

You begin to piece together what you missed moments before you arrived. A man named Jeremiah, son of Hilkiah, came to the entrance of the temple and began to proclaim a message that he said was from Yahweh to all the people of Judah who were coming to worship at the temple. If Yahweh has something to say, then we need to listen. As people begin to fill you in on what you missed you hear more pieces of the message that Jeremiah proclaimed:

> This is what Yahweh Almighty, the God of Israel, says: Reform your ways and your actions and I will let you live in this place. Do not trust in deceptive words and say, "This is the temple of Yahweh, the temple of Yahweh, the temple of Yahweh!" If you really change your ways and your actions and deal with each other justly, if you do not oppress the foreigner, the fatherless or the widow and do not shed innocent blood in this place, and if you do not follow other gods to your own harm, then I will let you live in this place, in the land I gave your ancestors for ever and ever. But look, you are trusting in deceptive words that are worthless.
>
> Will you steal and murder, commit adultery and perjury, burn incense to Baal and follow other gods you have not known, and then come and stand before me in this house, which bears my Name, and say, "We are safe"—safe to do all these detestable things?...
>
> Go now to the place in Shiloh where I first made a dwelling for my Name, and see what I did to it because of the wickedness of my people Israel... Therefore what I did to Shiloh I will now do to the house that bears my Name, the temple you trust in, the place I gave to you and your ancestors. I will thrust you from my presence, just as I did all your fellow Israelites, the people of Ephraim [the northern ten tribes].[21]

You remember stories of Shiloh. You remember hearing about how Israel's enemies came in and destroyed Yahweh's "dwelling place." They smashed it to the ground, and now this Jeremiah is saying that the same thing is going to happen to the Jerusalem temple? Your only response is a blank stare, a wide open mouth, and the hot flush feeling of angry blood running to your cheeks.

---

21. Jeremiah 7:3–15. See also Jeremiah 26.

Jeremiah has brought to light the reality that there are some of Yahweh's people who have placed their religion over human beings. They have forgotten why they even go to the temple in the first place. The temple was supposed to be the place where Yahweh's people (a people driven by the life-giving commandments of their covenant) are empowered to be more who Yahweh wants them to be. But now it has become a religious "home base" where selfishness and entitlement dominate. Those who were supposed to be on the side of the poor, the foreigner, the oppressed, and the most vulnerable have abandoned Yahweh for religion.

So now, Yahweh will destroy the beautiful structure that bears Yahweh's name right in front of the people who cherish it the most.

This Jeremiah is not done yet, he's just getting warmed up. Apparently Jeremiah has another message for the people from Yahweh, but this time the people are listening with cynical and angry ears:

> This is the word that came to Jeremiah from Yahweh: "Listen to the terms of this covenant and tell them to the people of Judah and to those who live in Jerusalem. Tell them that this is what Yahweh, the God of Israel, says: 'Cursed is everyone who does not obey the terms of this covenant . . . Obey me and do everything I command you, and you will be my people and I will be your God' . . .
>
> 'There is a conspiracy among the people of Judah and those who live in Jerusalem. They have returned to the sins of their ancestors, who refused to listen to my words. They have followed other gods to serve them. Both the house of Israel and the house of Judah have broken the covenant I made with their ancestors.'"[22]

As if attacking the temple, the central symbol of Yahweh's presence, is not enough, now Jeremiah is saying that the covenant that Yahweh made with the people is broken because they abandoned Yahweh and Yahweh's way for another way of living. In other words, Yahweh's wife has cheated on him.[23]

Remember the tassels? Remember how they were supposed to remind the people of Yahweh's fierce love and nurturing care? That is what

---

22. Jeremiah 11:1–10.

23. See Jeremiah 2–3 for an expansion of this marriage metaphor, including the part where Yahweh calls the people a whore.

Yahweh's commandments were, Yahweh's loving invitation to embrace a way of living that is more authentically human than the ways of living that the other gods promoted. One ancient god named Molech required a ceremony of his followers where you would take your firstborn and sacrifice them in fire.[24] This would show Molech just how devoted you were to him. Yahweh gave Judah a choice: live in a covenantal relationship with Yahweh by embodying the way Yahweh instructed, or choose to follow the ways of these other gods. It was Judah's choice, and as a result of their choice the covenant was broke. Yahweh's commandments were abandoned. Their marriage with Yahweh ended in divorce.

Imagine how disturbed you would be if two pieces of your culture, let alone two pieces that were central to your culture, were said to be null and void. How angry would you be? How would you express your opposition to the person who just announced those messages? But what if that person didn't stop there, and so boldly kept speaking of your nation's demise?

What if you were Jeremiah? What if you had to speak these harsh words of condemnation to your own people? You are a resident of this nation that you are speaking against so fiercely. Your fate is somehow inextricably linked to the fate of your people. The temple is important to you and your family too. The covenant with Yahweh is central to how you understand your place in the world. Would your family disown you? Would your friends abandon you? How lonely would you feel?

Jeremiah has more to say:

> This is what Yahweh says: Look! I am preparing a disaster for you and devising a plan against you. So turn from your evil ways, each one of you, and reform your ways and your actions.[25]

Jeremiah urges and pleads with the people to turn from their destructive behavior with the hope that if they do they will avoid the disaster that Yahweh has prepared for them. Jeremiah's urging, however, is intensified by something Yahweh showed him right before he delivered his message.

---

24. 2 Kings 23:10, Jeremiah 32:35.
25. Jeremiah 18:11b.

Yahweh told Jeremiah to go to a potter's house, and from there he will receive the next message. While there he saw something that changed everything:

> So, I went down to the potter's house, and I saw him working at the wheel. But the pot he was shaping from the clay was marred in his hands; so the potter formed it into another pot, shaping it as seemed best to him.
>
> Then the word of Yahweh came to me. He said, "Can I not do with you, house of Israel, as this potter does?" declares Yahweh. "Like the clay in the hand of the potter, so are you in my hand, house of Israel. If at any time I announce that a nation or kingdom is to be uprooted, torn down and destroyed, and if that nation I warned repents of its evil, then I will relent and not inflict on it the disaster I had planned. And if at another time I announce that a nation or kingdom is to be built up and planted, and if it does evil in my sight and does not obey me, then I will reconsider the good I had intended to do for it.[26]

Yahweh lets Jeremiah know that it is Yahweh's choice as to what nation can be used for God's purposes, and depending on what the people do will depend on how Yahweh will react. Wait a second, I thought it was the nation of Israel that was "elected" as Yahweh's people to be a blessing to all? Now, in light of this potter metaphor, any nation can be chosen by Yahweh!? Israel's, and now Judah's, position as "God's elected people" is not so certain anymore. Who Yahweh chooses, is up to Yahweh.

Like a dagger to the heart, these words, and the potter metaphor, would be too much for this people. Their whole existence depended on being Yahweh's chosen people to lead the revolution of healing and restoration in a world that was broken. Now, that is all null and void?

If you and I were residents of the nation of Judah when these words were spoken, we would have lost all hope. This would have been the last straw. All is hopeless, all is for naught, it cannot get any worse than this . . . or can it?

What is left of this tattered nation? The symbols and stories that gave Judah her identity have been dismantled by the words of Jeremiah. What if the words Jeremiah speaks actually happen?

---

26. Jeremiah 18:3–10.

No worries, because we still have our king. Our king is a symbol of strength and hope, a symbol of strength because he is a leader that we trust. He has chariots and fine palaces filled with nice things. A symbol of hope because the king is the person charged with the task of embodying Yahweh's instructions, and by following Yahweh's instructions he shows us how to uphold our end of Yahweh's covenant. Yes, we have our king, he is still in charge, maybe all is not lost.

Then, yet again, Jeremiah speaks up:

> Hear the word of Yahweh to you, king of Judah, you who sit on David's throne—you, your officials and your people who come through these gates. This is what Yahweh says: Do what is just and right. Rescue from the hands of their oppressors those who have been robbed. Do no wrong or violence to the foreigner, the fatherless or the widow, and do not shed innocent blood in this place.[27]

Sounds good so far. This is the business that is supposed to define the king. Justice and righteousness, as defined by caring for the most vulnerable, are the mandates of our king.

However, Jeremiah is not done, and this time he claims to be speaking Yahweh's words:

> "Woe to him who builds his palace by unrighteousness,
>   his upper rooms by injustice,
> making his subjects work for nothing,
>   not paying them for their labor.
> He says, 'I will build myself a great palace
>   with spacious upper rooms.'"
> So he makes large windows in it,
>   panels it with cedar
>   and decorates it in red.
>
> "Does it make you a king
>   to have more and more cedar?
> Did not your father have food and drink?
>   He did what was right and just,
>   so all went well with him.
> He defended the cause of the poor and needy,
>   and so all went well.
> Is that not what it means to know me?"
>   declares Yahweh.

---

27. Jeremiah 22:2–3.

"But your eyes and your heart
>   are set only on dishonest gain,
> on shedding innocent blood
>   and on oppression and extortion."[28]

Therefore, Yahweh says:

> "Though you are like Gilead to me,
>   like the summit of Lebanon,
> I will surely make you like a wasteland,
>   like towns not inhabited.
> I will send destroyers against you,
>   each man with his weapons,
> and they will cut up your fine cedar beams
>   and throw them into the fire."[29]

Even the king, the one who was supposed to get it, has abandoned Yahweh's instructions for another way of living. A way of selfishness; a life defined by using wealth not for the benefit of those who are most vulnerable, but rather, to make his own palace bigger. *What hope do we have now?* If our very own king has failed and will fall, then what is left?

Our temple . . . the covenant . . . our position as Yahweh's chosen people . . . and now our monarchy, what if it all goes away? What will we do?

In the year 597 BCE the Babylonian army, led by King Nebuchadnezzar, marched toward Jerusalem. As the Babylonian army laid siege to the city, the king of Judah, Jehoiachin, surrendered to avoid further bloodshed. Judah was now, like in the stories of old, a slave. It was at this time that Nebuchadnezzar took the Judean king, his family, and his officials to Babylon as exiles along with many soldiers, skilled workers, and artists. Nebuchadnezzar appointed Jehoiachin's uncle, Zedekiah, as king of Judah.

In the year 587 BCE Zedekiah rebelled and the Babylonian armies came back to Jerusalem, except this time it was for keeps. They set up a blockade of the city until the people inside began to starve, and then they stormed the gates of Jerusalem. They ransacked the city burning it to the ground. Bodies of women and children polluted the streets, while

---

28. Jeremiah 22:13–17.
29. Jeremiah 22:6b–7.

their blood pooled in the potholes. The royal palace was destroyed. The temple, the centerpiece of Judean culture and worship, was looted by the Babylonian army shortly before they burned it to the ground. The king's children were killed before his eyes, and in a twisted display of power, they gouged out the king's eyes so that the last image he would ever see would be the lifeless bodies of the children he loved. What was left of Judah's inhabitants, except for the most poor and vulnerable, were taken into captivity and led to Babylon, where they would make their new home.

No longer were Jeremiah's words just words. Everything was gone. What was once the city of Yahweh's people was now no more than a pile of ashes, rising smoke and death.

Movement 2

The Moment of Inescapable Waiting

3

Black Thursday

"No doubt it would be easier to navigate through the wreckage with safe categories, with answers rather than questions. Yet, few are given at this point and the best one can do is to 'live the questions.'"

—Louis Stulman

ADRENALINE PIERCES MY NERVES as I figure out how I can fix this situation. I am convinced it is a nightmare, and before long I will awake safe in my bed with the comforting smell of Mom's breakfast filling my room; but since I am dreaming I might as well pretend this is real.

So, I turn and run back into my house, yelling. Something happens as I run. Every step I take jolts me more awake than the step before. By the time I reach the phone I realize that I'm . . . not . . . dreaming. In spite of my awakening, I can still fix this, I can still make it o.k. This will all be better soon.

In five minutes I'm surrounded by strangers who care, but don't. Their presence confirms what I didn't want to believe: I can't fix this. I cling to my brother. The only human in the world who feels what I feel right now. Maybe I cling to him because subconsciously I don't want to lose him too. The strangers approach us and explain that they want to take us somewhere else. They put me in one vehicle and him in another. I get scared because I am alone. The car drives away, away from my home, away from my brother, away from my mommy and daddy.

A couple of hours have passed and I find myself sitting in Lee and Laura's living room with my brother and a few others. The room is cold and silent, and I am convinced that this must be a different room than the one I've sat in dozens of times with my friends. The living room I remember was bright and warm, it smelled of delicious food and life and refreshment. But this room is gray and void of any feeling, a cathartic space in between the dream world and the real world.

It is into this silent haze that the loneliness enters. I am startled by its presence. I have never lacked the presence of friends, and if I ever found myself in a situation where I did not know anybody my gregarious personality would quickly tilt the scales in my favor. Here, though, I am defenseless. Some of the closest people in my life are sitting in this living room, but the only voice I hear is the loneliness forcing itself upon me. The content of its speech is more than just being alone, it is a feeling of emotional and mental isolation, and before I know it I am engulfed in a cage of utter despair. Like in a dream where I am trying with all my might to scream, but nothing comes out. As I lie on that living room floor the only noise that escapes the cage is an exhausted weeping.

❧ ❧

"Chris, Laura and I think you and your brother should stay here for a couple of days until we figure out what is next. But to do that we have to go get the two of you some clothes from your house. Can you do that right now?" At this point my decision making abilities are, like my entire being, paralyzed. I say yes because that seems like the right thing to say.

Dean and I climb into the backseat of the car, and Lee and Sam get into the front. It isn't until about halfway through the drive that I realize what we are doing. We are going back to the same house, the same garage that I walked out of this morning. I can't do that, not now, not ever. If I had any energy to protest I would. I am forced to trust Lee and Sam although everything within me is screaming "No!"

Night has fallen. We arrive at the house where I grew up for a good part of my childhood, and everything is dark around us. The details of the outside that I grew to know so well, the tall windows, the peaked roof, the manicured landscaping, are all muffled in the thick darkness. But I can make out the garage perfectly. Lee helps me out of the car and guides me toward the door of my home. I understand the mission of this trip: go in, get some clothes, and get out as soon as possible.

Lee opens up the door in the garage and we walk in. It's almost as if the house has been waiting for me all day, waiting for this moment to pounce. As soon as I enter the kitchen I am inundated with memories and pictures. Mom baking Christmas cookies. Dad sitting in the next room watching the news while reading a book. Max, our dog, running around vying for everyone's attention. Birthdays. Graduation parties. Sleepovers. Thanksgiving meals. Celebrations. Fights. Yelling. Crying. Loneliness. The memories are crushing my soul and I collapse on the kitchen floor and wail.

I am not on the cold linoleum very long until I feel hands and arms surround me. They gently rub my shoulders and back, and then slowly but steadily begin to lift me to my feet. They support most of my weight as we start to make our way upstairs to my room. I sit on my bed as Lee grabs clothes from my closet and puts them in a bag. He then resumes his position next to me and leads me down the stairs and back to the car. As he helps me into the backseat I glance up at his face and see that his eyes are watery and red too. I haven't had the chance to think about anybody but myself yet today, but for a brief moment I feel sad because my friend has been crying.

We arrive back at Lee's house and my brother and I make our way inside. As we enter the living room I lift up my eyes to a sight I can't quite comprehend. People are everywhere. There are people sitting on couches and seats. People standing against walls. People leaning on tables. People peeking around corners of rooms. I feel their eyes with the same intensity that I felt the memories from my house just an hour before, except this time their eyes feel good. For the first time since the nightmare started I feel safe.

Something happens inside of a human being when they are literally surrounded by the presence of people that care. That feeling I felt when Lee picked me up off of my kitchen floor and led me upstairs, the feeling of having my weight supported when I couldn't support myself, that is the feeling that overwhelms me in this familiar living room.

In the next moments my brother and I are hugged and touched by what seems like an endless flow of people. Words aren't spoken, and if they are then I don't even process them. What I am conscious of is the transformation of the living room. Out of all the places in the world right now, this is where I want to be. Because at least for these few moments the loneliness has left the building.

It doesn't take long for the valium to start working and I feel my body drifting closer to sleep. Somebody, I don't know who, takes me by the arm and slowly leads me up the stairs to the bed I will call mine for a couple of days. I am barely conscious enough to feel their hands grab the sheets, pull them up over my shoulders, and then gently rub my back. "Goodnight my friend." How Drew traveled from Ohio to Indiana so quickly I don't know, but his voice assures me that my friend is here. With his words still lingering in my head I gladly welcome the numbing effect of sleep.

It is a couple of days later and after a blur of activity I find myself back at my own house. For reasons I can't explain, my house is filled with people. Most of those who are present are friends from high school, friends that are used to seeing me in a state of confidence and energy, neither of which I possess right now. That is o.k. with me, though, I am just glad they are here.

"Here Chris, why don't you put the lights on," Dean hands me the boxes of red Christmas lights, the same lights that Dad put on our tree year after year, every year looking more perfect than the one before.

When I finish I step back and look at the glowing red tree. I turn to leave because the red lights begin to pierce my soul when Dan wraps his arms around me. Dan grew up down the street from me, and we share quite a number of memories together, most of them legal.

"Chris, I'm so sorry. I'm so sorry." I have lost count of how many times I have heard those words over the past three days, but something in the shakiness of his voice confirms the depth of their meaning.

"They would have been so proud of me, Dan. I think I got all A's," referring to my first semester of college. Dan was one of our high school's valedictorians, and he always knew that I was capable of better grades than what I achieved in high school. His arms held me tighter after I told him that, and for a moment I closed my eyes and felt safe.

Faces and memories fill my sight for the duration of the evening. We put ornaments on the tree, and Mom's bows. As the evening winds down my friend Jon pulls me aside, "Listen Chris, I will stay here with you if you want me to. I'll stay for as long or as little as you want. If you want me to sleep next to you I will." A deep caring seeps from his words, a care that I want to trust.

"Please stay with me Jon. Please stay."

※ ※

The normal cycle of life, so I was told, proceeds like this: you are born, you grow up, you get married and start a family, your kids grow up, and then sometime after all that has happened your parents die. This is what I came to expect growing up. When I entered college I assumed I was somewhere toward the final years of the growing up stage and would soon enter stage three. No one taught me what to do when stage five sticks itself in at the end of stage two.

But that is the reality of suffering isn't it? It enters in as an uninvited guest into the plans of our life, and that interruption throws everything else out of whack. I had never entertained the thought of what life would be like without my parents. My imagination didn't have categories for that. When they died I felt as if somebody threw out the script that was my life and all of a sudden I had to improvise. Improvisation is not one of my strong suits.

All of the events I had imagined before they died (playing football in college, graduating from college, Dad's retirement, my search for a vocation, getting married, having children . . .) were all of a sudden erased from my memory. What remained was a pile of blank pages where these future memories used to occupy. How could I go through my college graduation without my parents being there to celebrate? How could I have my wedding without their presence? How could I hold my children in my arms knowing that their grandparents never would? What do I do with all of these questions? Everything changed. Everything.

Death isn't the only type of suffering where this interruptive change occurs. Any experience of suffering changes us and our future: a broken leg, diabetes, divorce, a house fire, the deterioration of a close friendship, sexual abuse, a denied application, a terminal diagnosis, loss of a job, victim of burglary, and the list goes on and on and on. The point isn't how big or small the suffering seems to be, the point is that everything changes.

"Are you cold? Do you need anymore blankets?"

"No, I'm fine. Thank you, Jon. I mean for being here all this time, thank you."

"Chris, you don't need to thank me, you would do the same for me. Just lay down and rest, tomorrow is a big day. I will sleep right here next to you, if you need me for anything just tap me and wake me up."

"What about the others that said they were going to sleep here? Do we have room for them too?"

"Plenty. They'll have room on the floor around us."

"O.k. Will you help me spread out these pictures of Mom and Dad on the coffee table so they can be next to me when I sleep?"

"Let's see what you got." I delicately hand Jon a few pictures to spread out next to those that I've already set out. This picture ritual has been a consistent part of my going to bed routine for the past couple of nights. For reasons I can't explain it calms and soothes me knowing that their pictures are right next to me. It is the closest I can come to being in their presence again.

As we finish displaying the pictures I hear the rumble of footsteps coming down the basement stairs. Half a dozen of my friends emerge with pillows and sleeping bags in their arms. They have been here all through the evening, and, like Jon, told me that they were going to stay with me tonight. Many of them knew my parents well, and a few of them will be carrying their caskets in the funeral tomorrow.

"I couldn't believe how many people came to the viewing today. That really shows how loved and respected your parents were. If that many people show up tomorrow then there is no way they will have enough seats. People are going to be standing against the walls. Did you finish writing what you are going to say?"

"Yeah."

"I'm sure it will be beautiful, Chris. Just sleep now, you are safe. We are all here with you."

Jon is right. I feel protected by the presence of my friends who literally surround me on the floor of my basement. Protected from fear, protected from loneliness and its soul-crushing capacity, protected from the nightmares that are just waiting to ambush me in my sleep. At least for this night I can rest.

As I settle down onto my makeshift cot of blankets and pillows I feel an arm drape itself across my back. It is that arm that ushers me into sleep on this weary night.

※ ※

Just six days ago I was unpacking a car after completing my first semester of college. Despite the chaos of the past year and a half life was feeling pretty good. Now, less than a week later, I am standing in a room with family members from all parts of the country, waiting for my parents' funeral to begin. How could my life go from that to this? The whirlwind of the past week has left me numb. Thankfully, I haven't had any valium for two days.

My family and I walk out of the cramped room and into the large sanctuary where we will remember Mom and Dad's life. Hundreds of people have crowded into this space, and it is literally standing room only. I don't know if that gives me comfort at the impact their lives had on others or if it overwhelms me as I just want to curl up in a corner all alone. Whatever it is, my family and I take our seats toward the front and the service begins.

When it is time for my brother and I to speak we walk up on stage. I pull out the piece of paper I typed up in large font last night, and begin to read:

"How can I possibly put into words what my mom and dad meant to me, and the kind of people they were. How can I possibly share with you the unbelievable love that my mother and father showed to my brother and me?

"When I sat down to think of words to say about the two greatest people I have ever known, I came up with nothing. I have no words that can define the love, strength, and foundation that they stood for in my life.

"My brother will talk about the word greatness. I will simply attempt to define what my mom and dad stood for in all aspects of their lives . . . devotion. How does one define devotion? Is it endlessly giving of oneself for someone else's gain? If it is, then my parents far exceeded that realm. Look around right now, and I will show you the fruits of their devotion. It is evident on the many faces gathered here. It is evident in the tears that are shed today. It is evident in our entire family. It is evident in my brother and me.

"My parents loved us with all of themselves and then some. They continually gave to us until they just couldn't give anymore. They were devoted.

"They taught us to be devoted. First, to God, then to others. However, they didn't teach us this by words or lessons. We simply picked it up from the way they lived and how they treated others. For example, my parents devoted all of themselves to their friend Hazel, and her husband Hobart. They would strive every day to love them with everything they had, whether it would be a phone call, or a long trip. They were devoted. My brother and I now realize what devotion really is because of the examples we had. We long for the day when we can attempt to love our children as completely and perfectly as our mother and father did.

"My brother and I now enter this unknown stage called manhood. There is so much that lies ahead of us that we are a little weary to face, but we are not afraid. It is because of the devotion of these two wonderful people that we have no fear of the unknown ahead. Physically L. D. and Beverly Williams are gone, but their lives are not over. They will live with my brother and me for the rest of our lives. What they were, and what they ultimately became, is what my brother and I will strive for the rest of our lives.

"I want to end by recalling one of the favorite memories I have from my childhood. When I was little I would play outside for hours on end. No matter what task I was engrossed in I would always find great joy in collecting dandelions to give to my mom and dad after I came back in the house. Every time I presented my bouquet of yellow weeds to my parents they would hold them in their arms like they were a gift fit for a king and queen.

"To everyone else that bouquet was a just a bunch of weeds, but in the hands of my mom and dad it was something more. It is that love that I will take with me far into the future. That love will remind me of who I am as I walk the path that is my life. Even though my parents will no longer be with me, their love will guide me forward for years to come."

We walk down the steps and sit down by our family. I lean forward in my seat. With my head in my hands, exhausted, I weep.

Days passed and the time came to head back to college, even though everything within me didn't feel ready to resume life the way it was before.

But when would I feel ready? A couple more days, a week, a month, ever? My brother and I decided that we had two choices: pick back up the paths of our lives as they were before Mom and Dad died, or sit at home and continue to mourn. We told ourselves that sitting at home wouldn't be what they wanted. It must have worked because a couple of weeks after their funeral we packed our cars for our respective trips.

However, before we journeyed back to school we had one more day that none of us were looking forward to. A day that had always been a reason to celebrate, a day full of joy and gratefulness now loomed on the calendar almost taunting us that it was drawing near. The irony was unavoidable. How could my brother's birthday ever be the same again? Mom and Dad were the reason that he was even born, and now we had to figure out how to celebrate without them.

We chose to go to Hazel's house on Dean's birthday. Hazel was my mom's best friend. A couple of years earlier her husband had been diagnosed with lung cancer and my mom and dad chose to come alongside of her during that difficult time. They sat with them, made them meals, and drove them all over the country to his doctor appointments. When he died, Hazel found comfort in my mom's friendship, and as the years progressed they made more and more memories together. We had visited her house many times, but never in a situation of this complexity.

The large ranch style home looked like the setting of a birthday party. Streamers strewn across the dining room. People wearing multi-colored party hats with the annoying elastic bands that hurt if you accidently snap them on your chin. Half-eaten cake and ice cream left on disposable plates that say "Happy Birthday" in block letters. Balloons taped to chairs and ceiling fans and corners of tables.

Even with all of the decorations and ambience, I will never forget the feeling we all felt after we lit the candles and sung the song. Birthday wishes are supposed to create smiles not tears, and what happens when the one wish everyone wants to come true can't? I held my brother and we cried together, both of us fully aware that no matter how bad we wanted to escape the pain of the moment, we couldn't. Whether we liked it or not this was his 22nd birthday.

❧ ❧

"I don't know if I can do this for a whole semester, Dean. I miss them so much," my voice trails off as I begin sobbing. Uncle Kevin, Hazel, and

Christi dropped me off at school about two hours ago, but something about their presence with me and then their abrupt departure makes me feel alone and afraid. So, I called Dean hoping that his voice would bring me some comfort.

"I know Chris, I know. Just try to get settled for the evening, unpack your stuff and get something to eat. Then, call me again before you go to bed. I love you."

"O.k., I love you too." After I hang up my standard issue dorm room phone I lay on the floor hoping to regain some emotional strength. Uncle Kevin made arrangements so that I could have a room to myself for the term, which I am grateful for, I have no energy or desire to try and cultivate a healthy roommate relationship right now.

After a couple of minutes I get the courage to stand up and go to the boxes sitting on the desk. The built-in desk resembles a countertop that spans the width of my room. Since I don't have a roommate this term I decide to turn the extra desk space into a makeshift memorial. I open the boxes labeled "Mom and Dad" and begin to unpack their memory laden contents: stuffed animals, picture frames, knickknacks, old birthday cards, a football, jewelry, and mom's eyeglasses. Arranging these items becomes so therapeutic that everything else around me fades away. I become obsessed with the distance between objects, the angles of the picture frames, the symmetry of the display. It was as if by arranging these items in exactly the correct way I would bring the world back into the way it was supposed to be, no more pain, no more crying, if only I can get it right.

I complete the memorial to my satisfaction, and step back to the startling realization that nothing has changed. They are still gone, I am still broken and empty, the despair has not lifted.

Tears admitting defeat stream down their previously carved paths on my face.

I exit the room and begin walking down the hallway to the shared bathroom. Each step feels like a haze. I seem to be moving, but can't quite comprehend how. Half a dozen 18-19 year olds cease their conversations as I get closer. Their faces turn to me as their smiles fade into looks of solemnity. They are trying as hard as they can to express care as I pass them. One in the group says, "I'm sorry to hear about your parents, Chris." To which I lift my heavy eyes and meet his. I have no energy for anything more, but his eyes tell me that is o.k.

Black Thursday

No matter how much I miss her,
I know I can't call her.
The arms that once held me close
can't embrace me.
The lips that could soothe any cut or scrape
Will never find my cheek again.

So I put on my jacket.
The black leather surrounds me
as its warmth protects me.
Its embrace comforts me on the coldest of days
Just like his arms once did.
A gift from them that was so unexpected, but so purposed.

It's not the same, not at all.
But there is something in the understanding of it
that gives me rest.
I can go on; I can thrive
only because they loved me without ends or limits or bounds.

I dry the tears that saturate my heart,
and step out into the cold winter,
surrounded by my jacket.

The human brain is an amazing organ. When I sleep I don't think about breathing, my brain knows that I must breathe, so it tells my lungs to breathe. When I eat I don't think about contracting my jaw muscles to chew, or contracting my pharyngeal muscles to swallow (I don't even know what my pharyngeal muscles are), I just chew and swallow and my brain takes care of the rest. When I walk I don't think about trying to time up the precise movement of each muscle and leg so that I don't fall, I just decide to walk and my brain has learned over time what to do next.

But when we suffer deeply those automatic functions sometimes become less automatic. It was a cold February morning, which is a redundant statement in the Midwest, and I was supposed to go to one class before lunch. Walking to class should have been automatic, but this morning I didn't escape the despair when I walked out of my dorm room, and it paralyzed me. Every step I took from my dorm to that classroom felt awkward and forced. Like I was a toddler again having to strain with all of my focus to not fall on my face. It was in that moment that I learned what it meant to literally put one foot in front of the other.

After class I knew that if I went back to my dorm room I would lay on my bed and lose the little motivation I had at the moment to eat lunch. So, I pointed myself in the direction of the cafeteria and started walking, except this time I had a plan. I knew that the sidewalk I was on would eventually dead end into the cafeteria, so I looked down at my feet and started to walk. My left foot would move forward a bit, then my right. The rhythmic movement of my feet lulled me into a trance that I welcomed. As long as I didn't have to look past my next step then I didn't have to think about anything else. There may have been a piece of me that celebrated the amount of steps I took and the distance I had covered in spite of the despair in my soul, but all of that came to a sudden halt when I reached the doors of the cafeteria. To open the doors I had to look up, I had to look away from my feet.

The noise of the cafeteria threatened to overwhelm me until I saw Drew. Drew knew my schedule, and part of me believed he arranged pieces of his day around mine. He welcomed me to the table and took my backpack from me so I could go get some food. When I sat back down, Wes, who was a mutual friend of ours, sat down with us. We ate and talked, but I mostly just ate and listened.

I had grown accustomed to the heavy weight that I carried around with me the past couple of weeks. At first it seemed like an unwelcomed addition to my being, but after a while I just accepted it as a piece of me I couldn't escape. My stomach usually tipped me off to its presence, and something about the cafeteria or the food or Drew and Wes' friendship caused the feeling to escalate in my gut. I put down my fork, stared at the food on my tray, and knew what was coming.

When the weeping began I got up from the table and went to the bathroom. I cried incessantly, only finding momentary courage to look in the mirror at the broken person in the reflection. It wasn't long until the door opened and in walked Drew and Wes. They moved towards me with great intent not stopping until I was in Drew's arms with Wes' hands patting and rubbing my back. The crying was different now. It didn't stop when they entered, but with my head on Drew's chest I felt more free. I may cry, but the despair won't consume me as I do.

Black Thursday

Bam Bam Bam. "Chris, man, you in there?" Russ' voice is deep and strong, his knocking is even stronger. Part of me wants to get up off of the floor and open the door, but another part of me feels paralyzed and doesn't want to move. A good feeling arises inside because my friend cares enough to come check on me, but there is enough fear residing in my being that causes me to stay still without making a sound. Maybe it is the same fear that had kept me lying on the carpeted floor of my dorm room for the past two hours.

Bam Bam Bam.

It's not that I wanted to skip classes, which was becoming a regular occurrence. It's not that I wanted to skip football workouts, something I had never done in my entire football life. It's not that I wanted to make my friends think that I wasn't in my room when I really was. It's just that sometimes when I am in my room alone with only my thoughts for company, the thoughts win. I didn't choose to give in to the sad memories, I just did. I would have done anything to escape them. I had tried talking to one of the university's counselors. I had tried finding outlets for my emotions. Nothing I could do could get me away from the deep grief that had become my life. Crying helped for the moment, but the tears returned. When I was most down I would turn on "Gone Away" by The Offspring and kneel in front of my makeshift memorial and just cry. The music helped, but it didn't do what I so desperately wanted it to. It didn't take it all away. It didn't free me from my sadness.

So, I lay on the floor of my room, trapped. All I could do was wait. Wait for night to come where sleep sometimes gave me solace. Wait for the next meal which gave me a reason to get off of my floor and go somewhere. Waiting . . . waiting . . . waiting. Waiting in a prison of my own despair. How long would this last? How long would I feel imprisoned? How long would I feel that there is nowhere to go to escape? For now I'll just lie on this carpeted floor and grieve.

Bam Bam Bam. "C-dub, hey open up. Russ and I are going to dinner and we want you to come with us." Drew's voice echoes in the hallway outside my door. I freeze almost holding my breath so that neither of them will hear me. Maybe they'll think I'm gone.

Bam Bam Bam. "C'mon dub. Just open the door brother." But what would that help? Opening the door just means that I take my prison outside of the room with me, and whoever is in close proximity might find themselves behind the bars too. Opening the door won't make anything better.

Bam Bam Bam. "Dub, we'll wait here until you're ready to come out, but Russ is pretty hungry and I wouldn't keep him waiting too long. You know how cranky he gets when he doesn't eat on time."

I don't know how a smile crept on my face in this moment, but there it is. The sadness didn't go away, the weakness is still tangible throughout my body, the thoughts are still fresh on my mind, but for reasons I can't quite explain I am standing at the door unlocking the deadbolt.

※ ※

There is a repetitive pattern in my life that I've learned to live with. A pattern I can't escape. Thursday always comes whether I want it to or not, and every time I wake up and remember that it's Thursday I'm reminded of the nightmare that I lived through less than a dozen Thursdays ago. If I'm having a good week, Thursday is lurking around the corner waiting to pull me back down, waiting to remind me that it was on this day that death won and my suffering began.

So, I decided not to fight this unending cycle, and every Thursday I wear all black. Black pants, a black shirt, black socks, black shoes, black wristbands, even a black jacket. I don't quite know why I have chosen this ritual, why going throughout my day in all black actually makes the day more bearable, but it does. Maybe it's the outward expression to those around me that I'm still grieving. A reminder that although their lives may be treading along just fine I am still carrying around broken pieces of myself everywhere I go. Or maybe I wear black because it reminds me of what happened. If I start every Thursday dressed in my own wardrobe of mourning then I don't have to be afraid of being caught off guard by the sadness that is always on my trail. Or maybe my black dress is a middle finger to all of the clichés I have heard over the past three months. "Time will heal your pain." It's been almost three months and I don't feel any better, actually I feel worse. "Everything is going to be o.k." Everything is not going to be o.k. My parents will never see me graduate from college, pursue my dreams, be at my wedding, or hold my children. "You're going to make it through this, you're a strong person." If making it "through this" (whatever that means) depends on my strength then I might as well give up now. The reality is that I have no more strength left in my being, just sadness and exhaustion. "There is a reason for everything that happens." Does anybody really believe that there is some hidden reason why I woke up on a Thursday morning and found my parents dead? Because I would love to hear that reason. "God must have needed more angels in heaven." If some deity out there had anything to do with what happened to my parents on that cold morning, then I don't want anything to do with that god. Whatever the reason for my choice of clothing on Thursdays, no matter where I go or what I do, Thursdays are now all black. Not an assertive, hopeful, Johnny Cash all black, just black.

Should I be grateful for this repetitive pattern? Should I be happy that I have to revisit Thursdays every week? If life didn't cycle through days and weeks and months and years, would I be able to free myself from this deep pain? I was always taught that my life was like a long, straight road that I was traveling. That once I passed a certain point I would never have to return there again, just keep moving forward. If this were the case, then the intensity of my deep suffering would, in theory, lessen every step I took along that road. Instead, I am finding that my life is not a straight road, but a tortuous path with on and off ramps, u-turns, and forks. There may be some truth to the correlation of my healing and time passing, but that doesn't account for the reality that Thursdays will always come every seven days. More than that, though, Decembers will come once every year. No matter how many years I travel down the road of life, I will have to revisit December again and again and again. On December sixteenth of every year I will be reminded that tomorrow is the day that my parents died. I will remember the despair, the sadness, the horror. Will anything ever free me from this painful cycle?

I have no answers on this cold morning, all I have is black clothing. I put on my black socks, tie up my black shoes and walk out the door. This morning I have to be at the university's athletic center for an early football workout. Quite possibly the last thing I want to be doing right now, but then again I can't think of anything that I want to be doing this morning, so I might as well show up.

The workout is grueling and requires a physical and mental toughness that I don't possess. My goal is just to survive so I can go back to the safety of my room when it is done. About halfway through, though, I notice that my stomach is starting to imitate the unsettledness that I feel in the rest of my being. In the middle of Coach Akers' drill I realize that if I don't sprint to the bathroom I may ruin the space where we are currently doing this drill. I make it just in time. As I'm washing my hands my tired eyes find the mirror, and I feel very sorry for whoever is staring back at me on the other side. He is so pale that I wonder how he is eveb still conscious. I see through his eyes into his soul, and emptiness is the only word to describe what I see. The image makes me want to cry so I break my stare and walk out of the bathroom.

After the workout I just want to be alone. Showering doesn't even tempt me. When I arrive back to my room I curl up on the floor in my normal position, tired and weak. I have now become accustomed to the process of weeping and can sense the beginning stages: the welling up in my gut, the lump in my throat, the change in my breathing. I let myself progress through the stages, as I have no energy to fight them. The sobbing begins and I let it take me.

Fear and confusion grip me as I hear the door swing open quickly. I glance over, but don't move. I forgot to lock the door when I came in, and that realization pisses me off. But before the anger has a chance to well up Drew shuts the door and sits on the floor next to me. I am still lying on the ground when Drew's huge arms wrap themselves around me and drag me next to him. The smell emanating from his shirt tells me that he didn't shower either, he came straight to my room. As we sit there in silence I realize that maybe that's what I had hoped for all along, maybe that is why I didn't lock the door when I came in the room. Maybe subconsciously my mind knew what it was doing the whole time. I was waiting for someone to enter, someone to rescue me, to hold me, and in this moment being rescued feels good.

Comfort is a deceiving friend. I grew up comfortable; physically, emotionally, mentally comfortable. I bought into the "American Dream," a life where I am surrounded with wealth and I am entitled to anything I want. However, an unwanted side effect of the "American Dream" is the individualistic isolation it tends to cause. The more you pursue your own comfort, the more others are pushed out of your life. So, when life comes crashing down many find themselves hurting in a dark room all by themselves.

That is where I thought I would be too, cowering in a corner all by myself. But time and time again people around me entered into that dark corner where I was. They sat, they spoke, they hugged, they cried, they listened. Even the moments when everything inside of me wanted isolation, they still entered into the dark places. I don't know why they did. I don't know why Jon stayed with me countless days in a row, I don't know why Lee and Laura swept me up in their arms, I don't know why Drew kept knocking on my door, but they did. In a very real way they took the broken pieces of me and made sure I didn't leave any behind as I stumbled forward.

I had always been told that God put on flesh two thousand years ago as a Middle Eastern Jew, but in my darkest moments of despair it seemed that God put on flesh again and again in many different faces and names.

4

Weeping Alone ... Together

> "One by one they passed in front of me, teachers, friends, others, all those I had been afraid of, all those I once could have laughed at, all those I had lived with over the years. They went by, fallen, dragging their packs, dragging their lives, deserting their homes, the years of their childhood, cringing like beaten dogs."
>
> —Elie Wiesel

In the early 1990's the African country of Sierra Leone was engulfed in a brutal civil war led by the Revolutionary United Front (RUF), a militant opposition group opposed to Sierra Leone's established government. Over the next eleven years the RUF extended their violent attacks throughout the country, including the capital city of Freetown. Many were wounded, many died. Some estimates state that around 2 million people were displaced from their home country of Sierra Leone during the war, and lived in refugee camps in neighboring countries.[1] This was their only hope of escaping the violence that had overrun their homeland.

Many of these refugees found shelter within the neighboring country of Guinea. They left behind their homes, their possessions, their jobs, and sometimes friends and family. Some left in the middle of the night. Some traveled hundreds of miles on foot to escape the horror that was unfolding in their home country. These exiled peoples may have found physical safety in the country of Guinea, but living in a strange land, sleeping on a strange bed, and hoping that your family will find food to eat tomorrow is no way for a human to live. Scared and alone, many

---

1. See http://www.afrol.com/News/sil007_civil_war.htm, accessed November 14, 2010.

refugees sank into a deep despair. They had nowhere to go, nothing to do. All they could do was sit and wait for word that the violence had ended and the war was over. Then, they could go back home.

Refugee camps exist in many parts of the world for a variety of different reasons. Although the circumstances of the Judean exiles in the sixth century BCE were very different than modern day refugees I imagine that there were shared emotional experiences. I imagine both modern day refugees and the Judean exiles felt feelings of loss, anger, confusion, loneliness, and uncertainty about the future. Feelings that would paralyze any of us if we found ourselves in similar circumstances.

※ ※

When we left the Judeans everything they held dear had been stripped away, and Babylon's armies were leading large groups of captive Judeans on the long, arduous road to Babylon. There were two different deportations of Judeans to Babylon; the first was in 597 BCE and the second was in 587 BCE. It is the story of the first group of exiles that were taken captive in 597 BCE that will hold our attention from this point forward.

The city of Babylon is located approximately 600 miles Northeast of Jerusalem. However, the route that the Judean exiles were most likely led upon, the route that would have been easier traveled with a large group of people and animals, would have covered around 700–800 miles. A journey of that length, dependent upon the mode of transportation (walking, chariot, etc.), could easily have taken multiple months.

The length of the journey, though, might not be the most difficult obstacle. The geography and climate of the land between Jerusalem and Babylon would complicate matters greatly. The exiles would be led through vast, arid deserts where food sources were scarce and water even more scarce. Given that their path took them only 650 miles north of the Tropic of Cancer, a latitudinal distance roughly equal to the city of Phoenix, Arizona, temperatures during the summer months would have soared to dangerous highs. Rainfall would also be minimal, preventing the much needed cooling and refreshment for the travelers, both people and animals. The very young and the very elderly would have been at the greatest physical risk during a journey of this magnitude.

These complicated physical realities would only be magnified by the emotional and mental despair faced by this newly deported people. Imagine the shock that this first group of exiles must have experienced.

Some of these exiles may have had friends or family members killed by the recent Babylonian invasion. Then, without proper time and space for grief they were forcibly exiled. Even if their loved ones survived the initial onslaught of the invading army, they would still have to leave those loved ones behind as they were led away. Away from those they used to love, those who provided strength and support throughout the ups and downs of their lives. Thus, these exiles would have to learn how to grieve without those faces and voices that comforted them so many times in the past.

Along with the people that were left behind, the exiles would also leave homes, possessions, and resources that may have taken a lifetime to earn. Businesses that had been in the family for generations were abandoned. Farmlands that had been tilled, planted, and harvested by the same families for countless years were either taken over by imperial overseers or simply left fallow. Homes that provided a physical and emotional shelter were nothing more than a memory for those traveling the long road to Babylon. The comfort of the bed they slept in, the blankets used to keep warm on winter nights were now fleeting memories. Memories that only magnified the hurt and pain of their current circumstances. Every step they took away from Jerusalem increased their hopelessness and despair. Every mile accumulated by this deported people brought with it a greater sense of loss. What they left was now gone, what lay ahead was still unknown.

If the shock and denial that came with their disturbing reality did not wear off before they arrived in Babylon, then perhaps the overwhelming chaos of living in a strange land would cause it to cease. In Babylon, they were surrounded by strange architecture, strange cultural customs, and even a strange language. Blending in would not be an option for these new exiles. They stuck out to the residents of Babylon like the foreigners that they were. These Babylonian residents had different gods, different political structures, different agricultural practices, and different stories that defined how they saw the world.

There is one final observation that must be made if we are going to understand, as best as we can, the new residential reality of these exiles. There is no doubt that a deep sense of personal suffering accompanied each individual exile. It does not take a very empathetic person to realize the despair that would exist if they were in the same situation. The sense of *personal* loss would be immense. I lost "my" home, "my" friends, "my" life as I knew it. However, existing parallel to this sense of personal suffering would be a very tangible sense of *communal* suffering. This group of people not only experienced individual loss, but also, as was shown in chapter 2, great communal and cultural loss. Much of what defined this group of people in the world was gone. That loss was a shared experience among all of the exiles, an entire group of people experienced the same sadness. Just as entire communities, or even nations, lament great disasters,[2] this group of exiled Judeans had much to grieve together. Personal suffering and communal suffering were inextricably linked for these new Babylonian residents.

It was this suffering that compelled them to speak. They refused to allow their oppressors to silence them, and out of their deep anguish there arose poems that rejected acquiescence. Let us allow their voice, their own words, to bring a bit more vividness to what we have imagined so far.

> By the rivers of Babylon we sat and wept
> > when we remembered Zion.[3]
> There on the poplars
> > we hung our harps,
> for there our captors asked us for songs,
> > our tormentors demanded songs of joy;
> > they said, "Sing us one of the songs of Zion!"
>
> How can we sing the songs of Yahweh
> > while in a foreign land?
> If I forget you, Jerusalem,
> > may my right hand forget its skill.
> May my tongue cling to the roof of my mouth
> > if I do not remember you,
> if I do not consider Jerusalem
> > my highest joy.
>
> Remember, Yahweh, what the Edomites did
> > on the day Jerusalem fell.
> "Tear it down," they cried,
> > "tear it down to its foundations!"
> Daughter Babylon, doomed to destruction,
> > happy are those who repay you
> > according to what you have done to us.

---

2. The 2010 earthquakes in Haiti and Chile are recent reminders and examples of disasters that cause intense communal suffering.

3. Zion in this poem is another name for Jerusalem.

> Happy are those who seize your infants
> and dash them against the rocks.[4]

Perhaps this poem was written by someone who used to lead the people in singing songs to Yahweh in the Jerusalem temple. Or perhaps, the one who voiced these words watched the Judean musicians abandon their instruments as they arrived in Babylon. Whoever the author was, they began the poem with sitting and weeping, two actions, when combined together, paint a very clear picture of hopelessness and defeat.

Whether the hanging of the harps was an act of despair or insubordination to their captors' taunts is up for debate, but what is clear is that the songs which once gave this people life and perspective will no longer be sung. The question in the second stanza, "How can we sing the songs of Yahweh while in a foreign land?" illuminates just how severe the events discussed in chapter two really were. Confusion and intense fear have replaced their songs of joy. A fear so gripping that the poet is afraid that they will at some point forget their home city Jerusalem, and if they forget Jerusalem then they will have forgotten how good Yahweh had been to them, and if they forget that, then they might as well become Babylonians.

The poem ends with a persistent petition for revenge. It is quite interesting that the poem progresses from their forgetting to Yahweh's remembering, it is intriguing to note, however, that they do not ask Yahweh to remember them, rather they ask Yahweh to remember the wrong that has been done against them. The darkness of imagination in the last few lines causes me to pause, but not for too long, because I know the thoughts that have gone through my head when I have been wronged.

In its entirety this poem points to the very real, very deep pain that existed within these exiles. Not only are there hints of concern for what life would be like in this new land, but there is also a subtle concern lingering in the last stanza about Yahweh's presence in the midst of their pain. The poet feels compelled to remind Yahweh of how the Edomites taunted Judah after their downfall, but an obvious observation must be noted: the reason we remind others is so that they do not forget. The poet is more afraid that Yahweh will forget the exiles than the concern that the people will forget Yahweh. After all, every structure and symbol

---

4. Psalm 137.

that facilitated interaction with Yahweh is now gone for these people. Where is Yahweh to be found in their exilic suffering? Will Yahweh stay in Jerusalem, go to Babylon, or no longer be present at all? What if Yahweh forgets the people all together?

This theme of begging Yahweh to remember continues in another poem about the exile:

> Remember, Yahweh, what has happened to us;
> > look, and see our disgrace.
> Our inheritance has been turned over to strangers,
> > our homes to foreigners.
> We have become fatherless,
> > our mothers are widows.
> We must buy the water we drink;
> > our wood can be had only at a price.
> Those who pursue us are at our heels;
> > we are weary and find no rest . . .
> Joy is gone from our hearts;
> > our dancing has turned to mourning.
> The crown has fallen from our head.
> > Woe to us, for we have sinned!
> Because of this our hearts are faint,
> > because of these things our eyes grow dim
> for Mount Zion, which lies desolate,
> > with jackals prowling over it.[5]

This poem, also full of despair and hopelessness, begins with the same fear: what if Yahweh forgets us? The poet is so concerned with this question that he or she begins with two imperatives. This poet commands Yahweh to remember and look, and if you hear those words in a calm, pleasant tone of voice then you have misread the intensity of this literature. If this poem was texted through a cell phone or entered in an instant message box on your computer they would look like this: REMEMBER . . . LOOK. A pretty bold request given that Yahweh is the God enthroned as king of all creation. The force of these words is similar to the first time your three year old asserts their independence and demands you do something for them. What then happens is that the child is reprimanded for asking in a rude or impolite way, and taught how to express their request in a more appropriate tone. However, the poet here has lost all inhibition when it comes to politeness with Yahweh. The despair has

---

5. Lamentations 5:1–5, 15–18.

driven the poet beyond all rules of perceived, appropriate human-divine communication and instead fuels the fierce boldness of the language found at the beginning of this poem.

The rest of the lines of this poem expound why the despair exists. We must notice the use of first person plural pronouns throughout: us, our, and we. This deep pain is not simply an individualistically internalized experience. It encapsulates more than just the poet, but rather the entire group of people. So, the individual pain one feels in losing his father becomes a pain that the whole community feels. The loneliness and sense of loss a wife feels because her husband has been killed by the invading Babylonians becomes the community's loneliness and their loss as well. The crown upon their head, which alludes to their being chosen by Yahweh at Mount Sinai to be Yahweh's people, has fallen off. This pain penetrates all previously held beliefs about their identity and purpose in the world; it is a communal pain.

Although the immense personal and communal despair is evident throughout these texts, the poems in the book of Jeremiah acknowledge that it is not just the humans who know the pain of the Babylonian invasion and exile. Yahweh, too, is not removed from the experience of pain. Through Yahweh's own words we hear Yahweh's perspective:

> I have forsaken my house,
> > I have abandoned my inheritance;
> I have given the beloved of my soul
> > into the open hand of her enemies.[6]

These are words of lament, words of a parent or lover expressing deep grief at the loss of the beloved. Could it be that Yahweh is not outside of the grief and pain that exists within the exiles themselves? This was Yahweh's chosen people, a people that were intended to embody everything Yahweh was and is so that the rest of the world could experience the goodness of this God. Any parent who has had to watch their child make a destructive decision understands what Yahweh is feeling, or maybe it is the other way around, perhaps the pain of the parent originates in God's experience of heartache at the brokenness in the world. Abraham Heschel, one of the prominent Jewish scholars of the twentieth century, comments on these words this way:

---

6. Jeremiah 12:7, my translation.

Israel's distress was more than a human tragedy. With Israel's distress came the affliction of God, His displacement, His homelessness in the land, in the world ... But should Israel cease to be His home, then God, we might say, would be without a home in the world.[7]

When Yahweh's people are taken to Babylon, Yahweh grieves too.

Yahweh's grieving is even more evident in another poem from the book of Jeremiah:

> This is what Yahweh Almighty says:
> "Consider now! Call for the wailing women to come;
>   send for the most skillful of them.
> Let them come quickly
>   and wail over us
> till our eyes overflow with tears
>   and water streams from our eyelids."[8]

In this poem Yahweh calls for the professional mourners to come and grieve what has happened. What we cannot ignore as readers is that in this poem Yahweh uses first person plural pronouns: us and our. The wailing women are not just for the people, they are there for Yahweh too, and Yahweh does not want them to stop until there are tears flowing from Yahweh's eyes. Terence Fretheim says it this way, "The professional mourners are to come and weep not only for Israel, but for God as well! In some sense, God has died the death of these people; God, too, goes into exile."[9]

For the exiles and for Yahweh despair seems to be the prominent reality.

❖ ❖

As the exiles arrive in Babylon they are taken to the place they will now call home. Whatever items they may have carried on their backs from Jerusalem they set down. If this scene were in a movie there would be no need for dialogue, the look on their faces says it all.

The question quickly emerges, "What do we do now?" Because the reality is that no matter how far they travel from Jerusalem they cannot

---

7. Heschel, *The Prophets*, 142–43. See also Fretheim, *The Suffering of God*, 133–34.

8. Jeremiah 9:17–18.

9. Fretheim, *Jeremiah*, 162. See also Heschel, *The Prophets*, 143, and Stulman, *Jeremiah*, 104.

escape their pain and their suffering. How are these Judeans, who have recently lost everything that was dear to them, pick up their broken lives and move forward? Those lives, all the way from their daily routines to their annual pilgrimage festivals, were dictated by their commitment to living Yahweh's way in the world, but no matter how far they look in every direction, there is no temple of Yahweh here. There is no place for the priest to offer the sacrifices. If a few years go by will they even remember the stories of Yahweh that meant so much to them?

These happened to be the same questions on Jeremiah's mind. Even though Jeremiah was not taken to Babylon with these exiles, his thoughts were still with those who were led away. It is from Jerusalem that Jeremiah decides to write a letter to those taken to Babylon. A letter that might help calm the confusion and help answer some of the questions in their minds.

This letter was approved by Zedekiah, the current king of Judah, and sent to the exiles in Babylon about 7-8 years before Zedekiah rebelled against Nebuchadnezzar, the Babylonian king.[10] What in the world could Jeremiah possibly say to these exiled Judeans that might make any difference? Their hope, their identity, their everyday Judean lifestyles are gone. What words could anyone craft and deliver that might encourage these exiles to not give up, and to still live in Yahweh's way even in this strange land?

Because a brand new tension now exists for the exiles. Do they try to figure out how to live Yahweh's way in Babylon or do they simply assimilate into the Babylonian culture? Abandoning who they were would not be too difficult in this new place. They could simply forget their old ways and learn the customs and lifestyles of the Babylonians. It would be like a fresh start, and in some regards that would make things a lot simpler. What do they do? How do they live?

It is into this chaos that Jeremiah's letter enters and speaks:

> This is what Yahweh Almighty, the God of Israel, says to all those I carried into exile from Jerusalem to Babylon, "Build houses and settle down; plant gardens and eat what they produce. Marry and have sons and daughters; find wives for your sons and give your daughters in marriage, so that they too may have sons and daughters. Increase in number there; do not decrease. Also, seek the peace and prosperity of the city to which I have carried you

---

10. See Jeremiah 29:1–3, and Clements, *Jeremiah*, 170.

Weeping Alone . . . Together

into exile. Pray to Yahweh for it, because if it prospers, you too will prosper."[11]

These are the first few sentences in Jeremiah's letter.[12] If we step into the shoes of one of these Judean exiles and listen with their ears, then we will quickly hear that the language Jeremiah uses in these sentences is loaded with weight and meaning. Let us try to do just that.

BUILD HOUSES AND SETTLE DOWN

The imperative to "build houses and settle down" seems kind of simplistic. What else are they going to do? They have to live somewhere, and shelter is one of humanity's most basic needs. So, isn't Jeremiah simply encouraging them to take care of their basic needs?

To answer that question let us take a look at how the Babylonians understood building in their culture. As discussed in chapter two, every culture has stories they tell to help make sense of the world. The Babylonians were no exception, and a few of their stories are especially helpful in understanding how they viewed the world.

One story in particular is very insightful. It is an ancient Mesopotamian story that tells of the creation of the world. It was written in the Akkadian language, and is called *Enuma Elish*. (*Enuma Elish* is Akkadian for "when on high," the first words in the story.) This story was discovered in 1849 in Koujunjuk, Iraq by Austin Henry Layard. The copy that Layard discovered was made for Ashurbanipal, a great Assyrain King, who lived from 668–627 BCE.[13] His death came shortly before the Babylonians became the dominant empire in the Ancient Near East. So, it can be accurately deduced that this story was in circulation before and during the time when the Judeans were exiled to Babylon.

In *Enuma Elish* there is a great battle among the gods to see who will reign as the chief of the gods. Marduk, who is an offspring of the champion gods, arises and is named the chief of all gods. Marduk realizes that a lot of work must be done on the earth, and so he decides to create human beings to do the work:

---

11. Jeremiah 29:4–7.

12. Although the main body of the letter is intended to be the voice of Yahweh, I will continue to refer to the phrases and language as Jeremiah's, since in essence the prophet speaks for Yahweh.

13. Benjamin and Matthews, *Old Testament Parallels*, 11.

> Blood I will mass and cause bones to be. I will establish a savage, "man" shall be his name. Verily, savage-man I will create. He shall be charged with the service of the gods That they might be at ease![14]

Therefore, in *Enuma Elish* human beings are created to work and build so that the gods may rest. There is no sense that the gods in *Enuma Elish* create humans out of love or compassion. In this story, human existence is equivalent to a pack animal.[15]

Another important story for the ancient Babylonians is referred to as the *Atrahasis Epic*. In this story the greater gods command the lesser gods to do the work of taking care of the world and creating canals (the canals were necessary for agricultural production). The lesser gods rebel, and Ea-Enki, the chief god, negotiates a deal with them:

> Summon Nintu, the divine midwife! Let her create workers to labor for the divine assembly . . . Create workers to labor for us. Let the workers bear the yoke, Let them work for Enlil, Let them labor for the divine assembly.[16]

Similar to *Enuma Elish*, in the *Atrahasis Epic* human beings are created so that they can do the work for the gods so that the gods may rest. In both of these stories the creation of human beings is simply a divine wish for a bunch of workers and builders. There is no sense of compassion or care for the workers, they are simply made to produce so that the gods can kick back and relax. This is how the Babylonians understood their place in the world when it came to building and working.

But how did the exiled Judeans understand the task of building? Was their perspective any different from the Babylonians? A quick glance at the creation story they held dear will help give us some insight. The ancient Hebrew story of creation begins with a god who creates human beings in God's own image as the climax of what has already been created. God then gives humans the responsibility of caring for the rest of creation, a creation which God approves of as "good."[17]

The very next chapter of the Hebrew Scriptures gives another account of creation, this time from a more human centered perspective. In

---

14. Speiser, "The Creation Epic," in *The Ancient Near East*, 36.
15. A point clearly articulated in Middleton, *The Liberating Image*, 166–67.
16. Benjamin and Matthews, *Old Testament Parallels*, 34.
17. See Genesis 1, God labels creation as "good" seven times in Genesis 1.

that account God looks at the earth and sees that, "there was no one to work the ground."[18] So, God takes dust from the ground, forms a man, and then breathes life into the man. A couple of verses later God takes the man and places him in the garden with a job to do. The man is supposed to, "work it and take care of it."[19] A simple observation must be made at this point, who in this story could do a better job of working and taking care of the garden, humans or God? Personally, I would choose God 10 times out of 10. The radical concept articulated in this story is that one way to image God in the world is to work with creation to develop something new, and this is a task intended to bring enjoyment. If the humans do not work and take care of the garden then it will stay stagnant, which is apparently not God's desire. Instead, it is hoped that the man, and eventually his female partner, would interact with the creation to develop something that was not there before. When humans work with creation to bring about something new we refer to it as culture. It could be art, technology, festivals, business, construction, etc., culture is what happens when humans work with creation to create. In the creation narratives of Genesis, human beings are intrinsically culture creators.[20]

This idea of working with creation to create something new continues throughout the early stories of the Hebrew Scriptures. Genesis 4:17 narrates that after the birth of Enoch, Cain built a city. Cain took the "materials" of creation and developed them into structures that eventually constituted a city. Or as my three inquisitive children ask, "Daddy, did God make that house?" To which I reply, "No, God made the materials, and human beings put it together." This culture forming continues in Genesis 10:11 where the city of Ninevah is built, and also in chapter 11 with the building of the tower in Babel (the prime example of what happens when culture formation goes wrong).

We must also make the observation that in the Hebrew creation story, culture formation is a communal experience. It was to the man *and* the woman that the first instructions were given to take care of creation. This is also why the first humans are told to reproduce, because the more "image of God bearing" humans there are the more they can work with

---

18. Genesis 2:5.
19. Genesis 2:15.
20. Middleton and Walsh, *The Transforming Vision*, 54.

creation to take care of it.[21] According to Genesis, creation of culture was an activity to be done with and shared by other humans.

So, when Jeremiah communicates to the Judean exiles that they are to "build houses and live in them" he is giving them an imperative to participate in the process of cultural development, which ultimately, in the Hebrew creation story, is a faithful acknowledgement of the image of God within all human beings. So, as they build their homes *together* they will find comfort and support in the midst of their grief. They will be reminded that building and creating is a gift from their God as they partner with God to take care of the world. Perhaps they will even find that building their homes with one another reminds them of God's presence. The communal experience of building their homes is intended to shine a bit of light and hope into the darkness of their suffering.

PLANT GARDENS AND EAT WHAT THEY PRODUCE

Before we take a look at the next phrase in Jeremiah's letter, it is important to make one observation. There is no way that Nebuchadnezzar, the king of Babylon, is going to allow uncensored mail to reach these new exiles in Babylon. His concern would be that the exiles, along with some outsiders, might plan a revolt against Babylon, and either try to escape or violently rebel. So, one way to make sure this doesn't happen is to censor any communication from the outside. This is why this letter was first sent to Nebuchadnezzar, before it was even allowed to reach the exiles.[22]

This should keep one point at the front of our minds: Jeremiah clearly does not want the exiles to become like the Babylonians, that would mean they would have to abandon Yahweh's way of living, but if he comes out in his letter and says that, then Nebuchadnezzar will destroy the letter. So, Jeremiah has to find creative ways to say what he wants to say to the exiles without upsetting Babylon's powerful elite in the process. Not an easy task.

The next phrase in Jeremiah's letter includes two verbs that are loaded with meaning within the stories and minds of the Judean exiles.

In the ancient Hebrew story of creation "planting" is a very important task. The first time planting is mentioned in the Hebrew Scriptures it is Yahweh who is planting a garden. Yahweh then places the newly cre-

---

21. Ibid, 55.
22. Jeremiah 29:3.

ated human in the newly planted garden.[23] Eventually, after the creation of woman, this primal garden becomes the dwelling place for the first human beings.

There are a few significant details about this first garden that we must note. First, it is a gift from God. The human beings did not plant the garden, it was God who planted it and graciously gave it to them as a dwelling. Second, the humans' needs were provided for within this garden. The garden became their primary source for shelter and food.[24] Finally, the garden is the first place where God and humans interact. The text of the story actually says that the humans heard, "the sound of Yahweh God walking in the garden in the cool of the day."[25] Before the temple, before the worship rituals of the Israelites, before anybody even prays to God, the garden becomes the first place in the Hebrew Scriptures where the divine and human mingle. It is important to note that this interaction with God in the garden does not occur until both man and woman have been created. In the garden, communing with God is a social, not individual, experience.

Therefore, Jeremiah's imperative to "plant gardens" is so much more than a suggestion to pick up an outdoor hobby. The temple is gone. The central structure of union with the divine has been dismantled and made impotent, only to be destroyed a couple of years later when Babylon's armies return to Jerusalem. How can these exiles be formed in the way of their God when they do not even have a structure to mediate divine interaction? How can they connect with their God in the midst of their deep suffering? According to Jeremiah it is by reminding the exiles of their ancestral garden homeland and the reality that a garden is where humans and God first interacted. The Babylonians may be able to hold the people captive hundreds of miles away from their land and temple, and thus cut the people off from their God, but maybe, just maybe, if the exiles plant some gardens they will find that Yahweh will come and take a stroll with them in the cool of the day.

"Eating" is also a very dynamic phrase in the Hebrew Scriptures. Early on in the creation process God invites the earth to bring forth vegetation. The earth responds to God's request and brings forth different varieties of plants and trees. These plants and trees contain within them

23. Genesis 2:8.
24. Genesis 2:9.
25. Genesis 3:8.

seeds that will allow them to reproduce.[26] A little later in the creation story God gives this vegetation to the animals and humans as a food source.[27] So, the gift of food in the Hebrew creation story is a gift given by both God and the earth for the sustenance of the living creatures.

This is why the Israelites never took eating for granted. Every meal they ate, every crop they harvested was a reminder that God cared about them and provided for them. They did not cause the sun to shine. They did not cause the rain to fall. Thus, if the sun did shine and the rain did fall and their crops grew, then they blessed God for continuing to take care of them. Eating is primarily a celebratory act within Israel's story.

This view of food and eating as a gift was very different than the view held by the Babylonians. In numerous Ancient Near Eastern stories, the humans produced food *for* the gods, and then whatever was left over, the humans could eat.[28] Therefore, if you were a farmer in Babylon and had crops then you would take a percentage of your crops and offer it to the gods. That percentage could change based on what the religious leaders demanded or whether you thought the gods were finally happy with your offering. It could be twenty percent of your crops one year and fifty percent the next year. So, for the Judeans to eat fruit with thankful hearts from gardens that they grew in Babylon was a condemnation against Babylon's entire oppressive agricultural system, and a statement about how good Yahweh is to them, even in exile!

Throughout history and across cultures eating has always been a communal experience. At the most special moments in life (weddings, graduations, baby showers, celebrations) people gather around food as a way to commemorate the moment. Many cultures even have funeral dinners that serve as a way for the mourning to be together and continue their grief. Eating in that setting brings people together with the hope that a shared meal may bring comfort to the mourners. For Jeremiah to instruct the people to eat together is an invitation for the exiles to gather around a table and experience the sacred mystery that occurs when humans share a meal. Perhaps the more meals they eat together the more they will realize that they are unified in their experience of suffering, they are not alone.

26. Genesis 1:11–13.
27. Genesis 1:29–30.
28. Middleton, *Liberating Image*, 149–67.

MARRY

Marriage ceremonies all over the world are intended to be joyful celebrations, not solely for the couple getting married, but also for the community that gathers to celebrate. In our culture there is an option of being married before a justice of the peace, with no ceremony or guests, but a majority of people choose a full-fledged ceremony with all the trimmings, even a cheesy photographer. The reason we choose to invite others to our wedding is so that they can celebrate with us. Many of us could not imagine a wedding ceremony without relatives or friends present.

So, it is into the middle of this suffering people that Jeremiah suggests that they give their children away in marriage. How could anyone expect this group of people to want to celebrate something as joyful as a marriage given their present circumstances? Could a large communal celebration really benefit these suffering exiles? Apparently Jeremiah thinks so.

HAVE SONS AND DAUGHTERS . . . INCREASE IN NUMBER

This is such an interesting imperative. Why does Jeremiah feel that having children is an important enough command to include in his letter? Perhaps, like the other phrases, we can gain some further insight by looking into the stories that would have shaped how the exiles heard Jeremiah's words.

The word used in Jeremiah's letter for "increase" is the same word used in the ancient Hebrew creation story after God makes the first male and female:

> God blessed them and said to them, "Be fruitful and increase in number, fill the earth and subdue it. Rule over the fish in the sea and the birds in the sky and over every living creature that moves on the ground."[29]

Directly after God creates the humans he gives them the tasks to "subdue" and "rule." Without going into great discussion about the meaning of these verbs, the bottom line is that the humans are supposed to act on the earth in the same manner that God has acted, with generosity and compassion.[30] So, it makes sense why God would want the humans

---

29. Genesis 1:28.

30. Middleton, *Liberating Image*, 60. Middleton makes this point in a much more eloquent way.

to increase, the more humans that exist, the more people to be generous and compassionate to what God has created. This logic continues throughout the story of the Hebrew Scriptures, and the idea is always the same, the more humans living God's way, the better life will be for all.

Jeremiah's command to the exiles to have children and increase in number is a provocative statement when read in light of their history. The hope is this: the more faithful Yahweh followers that the exiles produce and raise up, the better life will be for everyone around them. Also, the more followers of Yahweh that exist in exile, the less the temptation to abandon Yahweh and live like a Babylonian.

A friend of mine who I work with recently had a baby. All who knew her were very excited for her and continued to pester her with questions as to how she was feeling and what the doctor said at the latest appointment. Then, the day came for her to have the baby and there was a buzz around our workplace. A couple of weeks later she actually brought her newborn baby into the store. She no more then walked in the door and three people swamped her asking if they could hold that beautiful bundle (yes, I was in that three). Only a newborn baby can do that. Only a child a few weeks old can bring people together at that speed and with that joy. Perhaps the Judean exiles needed to experience the excitement and joy of a newborn baby being in their midst. Maybe they needed to be brought together again, and maybe only a baby could do that.

SEEK THE PEACE . . . IF IT PROSPERS

The Hebrew word that is translated as "peace" and "prosper" in Jeremiah's letter is the word *shalom*. This word often gets translated into English as the word "peace," but that translation alone does not quite give the full sense of what the Judean exiles understood by the word *shalom*. When we use the word "peace" we often mean the ceasing or absence of conflict, but a better way to understand the Hebrew concept of the word is the sense of wholeness and completeness that God intended at creation. For example, if my arm is broken then my body is not experiencing *shalom*. If I have wronged somebody and they have not yet forgiven me then that relationship is not experiencing *shalom*. Living in *shalom*, according to the Hebrew Scriptures, is how God intended us to live, whole and complete.

So, why does Jeremiah encourage these exiles to seek the *shalom* of Babylon? What about that activity would bring hope to this suffering

Weeping Alone ... Together

people? Again, a look into the story that shaped this people may give us some insight.

Very early on in the Hebrew Scriptures the *shalom* with which God created the world is replaced by brokenness and despair. The world is not how God intended it, and God is determined to do something about it. As was discussed in chapter two, God comes to a man and tells him to leave everything, and when he does God will bless him and his family so that the rest of the world might be blessed through them. God's plan to deal with the loss of *shalom* is to gather a people, eventually an entire nation, whose sole mission in life is to embody the *shalom* that God originally intended for humanity. Keep in mind that God does not stop with just the man, but rather it will take many generations of this man's family to reintroduce *shalom* back into the world.

Seeking and embodying *shalom* is always a communal/social experience in the Hebrew Scriptures. The Judean exiles are no exception. For them to seek the *shalom* of Babylon they are going to have to do it with the support and participation of the entire exilic community. I don't know about you, but when I am faced with tasks that seem near impossible (like seeking the *shalom* of my enemies), I desperately need others around me encouraging me every step of the way.

Now that we have taken some time to unpack the first few lines in Jeremiah's letter, what are some of the common threads that are woven through those first lines? Perhaps we could start with the reality that every verbal imperative Jeremiah writes to the exiles is an invitation to participate in communal activities. Building homes, planting gardens, eating meals, celebrating marriages, having children, seeking *shalom* are all activities that require more than one person. This becomes even more evident in the original Hebrew language. *Every one of these imperatives in the Hebrew are in the plural!* In other words, they are commanded to do the tasks together, in community. The language of the letter leaves no room for doubt, the people are supposed to begin working and living in an intentionally communal way as they seek to make sense of their new lives and their suffering.

Nowhere in the letter does Jeremiah tell people to stop grieving personally. Nowhere does he say that individual lament is bad. I am sure that these people were a lot like you and me. They had their moments of breaking down. They sometimes found themselves weeping alone in a corner of the room. Jeremiah is not telling this suffering community to stop weeping alone. He's telling them to weep alone...together. Jeremiah encourages this intersection of the personal and communal suffering in a way that our culture has lost. He reminds them that you must not have one without the other. Hope emerges, for the exiled Judeans, through the community's commitment to walk together through their suffering. Imagine the personal weeping without the communal gardening, that would lead to further hopelessness and depression. Imagine the communal gardening without the personal weeping, that would be fake. These exiles need each other in their grief, and Jeremiah is trying to communicate that reality in his letter.

What makes these imperatives even more amazing is something he writes a couple of lines later in the letter:

> This is what Yahweh says..."You will seek me and find me when you seek me with all your heart. I will be found by you," declares Yahweh, "and will bring you back from captivity."[31]

Yahweh will be found? But I thought they were in Babylon, hundreds of miles from Jerusalem? I thought there was no temple of Yahweh in Babylon? So, how can Yahweh be found? Outside of the exodus from Egypt, this is quite possibly the most significant moment in the history of this people. Jeremiah is telling these exiles that Yahweh can be found within the intentionally communal life of Yahweh's people. This is a brand new idea in the history of Israel's story.

Although, archeologists and scholars are somewhat limited on the extant information from this exilic time period, many believe that it was in this setting that the synagogue was born.[32] For the first time in Israel's history, people would gather together at homes or other public places for communal worship. They would read the stories of Yahweh together to further understand what it meant to be Yahweh's people. They would offer prayers to Yahweh. Activities that used to only take place at the temple were now happening in places as common as someone's dining room. A group of people gathered together and unified in Yahweh became the new temple. Following Yahweh would never be the same from this point forward.

---

31. Jeremiah 29:10a, 13–14.
32. Meier, "Synagogue," 579–80.

It was in a despair filled refugee camp in Guinea that two of the Sierra Leone refugees, Reuben Koroma and Francis Lamgba, had an idea. If they began to share their talent and passion for music with others in the refugee camp, perhaps it would bring life and hope into a very dark situation. Despite tremendous adversity these two men began a journey that would eventually lead to the formation of the band Sierra Leone's Refugee All-Stars. This band not only shared music with those in their refugee camp, but they eventually traveled to other camps and destinations to play their music. Their music unified the people and gave them a common voice as they cried out in their intense suffering. As more people heard their music and came together an unexpected thing happened, in the middle of a Guinean countryside, hope was born. Refugees who previously were without any reason to think their lives would improve, all of a sudden began to imagine something new, something better. All because two men unified a people through their common voice of suffering.[33]

---

33. To learn more about this amazing story, and to hear some of their music, please visit these two websites: http://refugeeallstars-audience.fm/ and http://www.refugeeallstars.org/.

5

Suffering With

Carry each other's burdens, and in this way you will fulfill the law of Christ.

—Paul

I HAVE A FRIEND who came to me one day and said he wanted to talk. He began to express that he was carrying around a whole pile of hurt, and he didn't know what to do with it. His whole life he had been told that if you really love God then you won't ever be sad. When negative events occurred in his life the ensuing pain only brought him guilt. He tried to figure out what was wrong inside for feeling sad or down about negative situations. This abusive religious system led him to even more despair; he concluded that because he couldn't get through his suffering by himself, he must not love God, or vice versa.

So, one day we found a quiet place and sat down together. We took our chairs and pointed them towards one another so that when we sat down our bodies would be facing each other. My friend just started to talk, and I simply listened. He talked about his current pain and how it stemmed from the deteriorating health condition of a close family member. Up to this point he had not had the opportunity to put a voice to this pain. It had remained a silent suffering.

The more my friend talked, the more pain came out. Pain that was pushed down so deep inside of his being that he had never dealt with it, pain that had lived within him for years. He spoke of situations in high school that had scarred him deeply. One situation in particular was so painful that every year around the same date he would sink into despair, because revisiting that date meant revisiting the pain-filled memories. Sitting in those chairs, it all came out. He cried, and I cried with him.

I cried because it hurt me to hear what he had gone through. I cried because I couldn't imagine carrying around the pain he had for so long. I cried because I couldn't do anything to take his pain away.

After a while he lifted his tear stained face and said, "I don't know why, but I actually feel a bit better. I don't feel as hopeless as I did a few days ago."

I was grateful to hear those words, but I was also perplexed. Why did he feel better after just talking with me? Did the simple act of sitting with me and verbally throwing up actually help my friend? Did my sharing in his suffering, however brief it was, help him in some way? Did it really engender more hope? Because all I did was sit on a chair and listen.

My sister found out at the age of 34 that she would never be able to be a mother. All of her life she dreamt of being a mommy, and in one short doctor's appointment that dream was crushed. Her and her husband wept and grieved. All of a sudden the future they had imagined together was gone, and what was in front of them was unknown. After a year of processing and grieving they decided to pursue the possibility of adoption.

Shortly after the decision to adopt they joined an adoptive support group where they learned more about adoption, the emotional journey of a birthmother, as well as the range of emotions adoptive parents experience. It was within this group that my sister realized for the first time that her anger and sadness were o.k., that she and her husband weren't alone in their feelings. That realization, that they weren't alone, began the slow journey of healing. A journey that culminated in my sister and brother-in-law welcoming two beautiful, twin baby girls into their family.

In May of 1935 Bill Wilson, a promising financial consultant, grew tired of his endless battle with alcoholism and the detrimental effects it was having on his life. He had tried time after time to be free of his need for alcohol, and it seemed that he finally was making progress. However, after a routine business trip to Akron, Ohio, failed, Bill found himself craving alcohol once again.

While standing in the hotel lobby Bill realized that there were primarily two choices in front of him: 1) go to the bar, sit by himself, and most likely end up drinking to excess, or 2) reach out for help to somebody outside of himself. Bill chose option number two. He went to a church directory that was in the hotel lobby, and after several attempts to reach someone, he reached a minister. The minister connected Bill with someone who also had an internal struggle with alcohol, a physician from the Akron area who was a recovering alcoholic, and on May 10, 1935 Bill met Dr. Bob Smith. They shared their stories with one another, and in just a couple of weeks they were helping each other to remain sober. Through the shared experience of these two men a movement of recovery was born that would soon touch people all over the globe. What started out as a simple cry for help to a fellow alcoholic, after a few years, turned into a worldwide movement of men and women committed to helping one another be free from the chains of alcoholism.

Today Alcoholics Anonymous, also known as A.A., has close to two million members worldwide. These men and women come from all sorts of racial, socio-economic, and geographic backgrounds. They range in age from late teenagers to ninety year olds, but what binds them together is a unified commitment to remain sober.

Ask any recovering alcoholic and you will quickly realize that sobriety is so much more than a choice of the intellect. Although the intellectual choice is the first step, to maintain sobriety members of A.A. must organize their lives around the tenets of A.A. Those tenets are found in twelve steps that guide the recovering alcoholic through a journey of healing. A reading of the twelve steps leads to the observation that only first person plural pronouns are used throughout the steps. There is no "I" or "me" in the steps, it is only "we" and "us," because for the recovering alcoholic the sense of communal identity is absolutely central to recovery.

Accordingly, the process through those twelve steps is not intended to be experienced alone. Local A.A. meetings are held regularly where recovering alcoholics can come together to share their experience, strength, and hope from each other's common struggle. Along with attending meetings, A.A. members may also have a sponsor. The sponsor is a person that is further down the road of recovery and can be one more piece of support for the recovering alcoholic. No one at Alcoholics Anonymous is expected to achieve sobriety alone.

And to think that this worldwide movement we now call A.A. began with one man choosing to invite another person into his struggle and suffering.[1]

※ ※

Renee was a nineteen year old girl who found herself beaten and battered by what had been the painful story of her short life. Damaging abuse, painful childhood memories, and voices of worthlessness trapped Renee in a corner causing her to find defense mechanisms that literally left their marks on her body. When drugs weren't enough to dull the intense pain in her soul she would take a razor blade, often the same one used to cut lines of cocaine, and cut herself.

It was in the midst of this painful reality that Renee was introduced to a group of people through a mutual contact. This group of people didn't think that Renee's life was worthless or without beauty. They came alongside of her and agreed to take her to a rehab center, the first glimmer of hope. However, the rehab center found the fresh cut marks on her arm and determined her too great a risk. They refused her treatment. Hope began to dwindle yet again.

These weren't your everyday friends, though. They found out that Renee could check into a rehab center in five days, but five days for someone strung out on drugs is a long time. So, for the next five days they chose to be her rehab center. They surrounded her every minute of every hour. They took her to concerts, fed her, played games with her, prayed for her, and never left her side. Their constant presence and encouragement ushered Renee through the darkness of those five long days.

As they arrived at the treatment center Renee turned to her band of friends and said, "The stars are always there but we miss them in the dirt and clouds. We miss them in the storms. Tell them to remember hope. We have hope."[2]

※ ※

For the first eight years of our marriage my wife and I lived in northwest Ohio. The city we lived in had a reputation, and for good reason.

---

1. For more information on Bill Wilson or A.A. see their website at www.aa.org, or *Alcoholics Anonymous*.

2. To read more about Renee's story and the grassroots movement that was birthed out of it check out "To Write Love On Her Arms" at www.twloha.com.

It was seen as a city where the residents were primarily Caucasian and had money. If you didn't fit in either of those categories you were often viewed with suspicion or simply ignored as insignificant.

Another dynamic permeated the atmosphere of this city. There was a strong religious culture that expressed itself in strict religious observances, loyalty to a certain political party, and prayers of the privileged that sought to justify the comfortable lifestyles of many of the religious citizens. Successful churches were seen as the ones who built the most extravagant buildings. Thus, the latest fad was to attend the church that just spent over $3.8 million on a new facility. Even the local seminary raved about its brand new ten million dollar building project. Financial prosperity and God's approval seemed to go hand in hand.

When my wife and I and a group of close friends began to question the values of this religious culture we found ourselves ostracized by churches and other groups claiming to speak and act for God. Some of us were fired from positions within these institutions, some were discreetly forced out of the communities we were a part of, but all of us had been hurt deeply by people we thought we could trust.

It was into this deep hurt that we chose, one October afternoon, to gather in a living room together with the intention of talking through our hurt from the past and our hope for who we felt God calling us to be. Conversation ensued and at the end of our living room gathering we decided to meet a couple of weeks later to continue. After we met a couple of weeks later we decided to meet for dinner the next Saturday night to keep talking. Then, we decided to meet for dinner the next Saturday to keep talking. Before we knew it we were showing up at someone's house every Saturday night to eat, pray, read, and talk. Eventually, one of our friends brought a big clay pitcher and set it in the middle of the room. We decided to pool our money together so that we could take care of one another as well as those in need outside our Saturday dinners.

After a couple of months we began to realize that, just like the exiled community in Jeremiah, we had found healing for our wounds in the midst of our community of love. We still had our issues that presented themselves, and we certainly had to deal with our own brokenness and negativity, but overall we felt welcomed and accepted as we pursued God together. Somewhere in our eating together, in our vulnerability with one another, in our sharing of finances and resources, we found healing. Maybe another way of saying it is that through our communal lives together we became more aware of God's presence in our midst, and that presence made a world a difference.

❖ ❖

On October 2, 2006 an armed man entered a one room Amish School in Nickel Mines, Pennsylvania. He ordered the teacher and the boy students to leave the building. After an attempt by the boy students to stay with their female classmates they were forced out of the school. The armed man then proceeded to shoot the ten remaining female students, killing five and severely injuring the other five. As the police swarmed the school the gunman took his own life, ending the greatest nightmare this Amish community had ever faced.

As news of the attack reached the mainstream media the story quickly shifted from the horrible details of the attack to the group of Amish residents who just a couple of hours after the tragedy were visiting with the widow and family of the gunman. This group of Amish delegates expressed their forgiveness and support to the gunman's family as they grieved the loss of their husband and father. Media outlets quickly began to question the validity and authenticity of the Amish expression of forgiveness. They wondered how any human could genuinely offer forgiveness so quickly following such a deep and horrific tragedy? The media speculated as to the mental health of a group of people who could offer forgiveness in that short of a time.

What many Americans realized as the story spread was just how unfamiliar most were with the Amish culture and way of life. As a result, three scholars who were familiar with Amish culture chose to write a book to help outsiders understand why the Amish reacted the way they did to the Nickel Mines tragedy. They gave this description of what influenced these Amish men and women to do what they did following the shooting:

> We believe the answer lies in the communal nature of Amish life. In the Amish faith, the authority of the community overshadows the freedom of the individual . . . Contemporary American culture tends to accent individual rights, freedoms, references, and creativity . . . In contrast, the core value of Amish culture is community.[3]

---

3. Kraybill, Nolt, and Weaver-Zercher, *Amish Grace*, 92–93.

It is this exalted value of community, the authors explain, that allow the Amish to be formed in ways that promote a lifestyle of genuine forgiveness. In other words, without the communal culture, formation in the way of forgiveness would not be possible for these Amish men and women.

❖ ❖

I met Chad during the summer before his senior year in high school. I was introduced to him by a friend of mine named Oliver. A couple of weeks before we met, Chad had been charged with possession of cocaine. Since he was still considered a minor, he had been put on probation. This meant that if his record stayed clean for a couple of years then the incident with the cocaine would not be put on his permanent record.

Chad, Oliver, and I began to develop a deeper friendship over the next months and years. Our friendship provided Chad with support as he tried to learn how to make better decisions for himself and his future. Despite being in the "older brother" role of the friendship, I valued Chad and Oliver's relationship as much, if not more, than they valued mine. There was a spark of creativity and adventure in both of their lives that was contagious to all around them.

So you can imagine how our hearts dropped when a couple of summers after I met Chad we found out that he had left the state, which was a violation of his probation, and joined a group of people whose communal life centered around heavy drug use. Chad's probation officer contacted me numerous times, hoping each time that I had information regarding Chad's whereabouts.

One day I was sitting in my office at my workplace when Chad walked through my door. I hadn't seen or heard from him in months and it took me a moment to process that he was actually sitting in front of me. His appearance, and pungent odor, communicated that hygiene and personal care had not been high on his list for the past couple of months. Somebody familiar with Chad's situation alerted the authorities that he was back in the city, and as Chad was walking out of my office the police handcuffed him and took him away.

What proceeded was a long, drawn out process of jail time, court appearances, sentencing, and ultimately a couple of months in a minimum security prison. Chad asked me at the beginning of that long journey if I would come and visit him. So, I arranged my schedule around weekly visits with Chad in the county jail and eventually monthly visits at the prison. These visits became very meaningful to me, and I looked forward to the one hour every week that I would get to spend talking with my friend. Chad was like a brother to me, and I didn't want him to feel alone in his experience.

Visiting him at the prison became harder because of the distance I had to travel to see him, so in lieu of our weekly visits we exchanged letters on a regular basis. One of Chad's letters in particular expressed just how much our visits sustained him:

> Thank you for coming to see me this past week! I really look forward to seeing you and talking with you about whatever. Every time you come and visit me it reminds me that I'm not alone in this place. It's easy to think that you don't have anybody on your side here, but when you come to see me I know that you are with me through this, and that helps me to get through the day.

I didn't have a bunch of answers for Chad. Most of our conversations were just chit chat about daily life, but I realized after reading that letter that it was more than just chit chat to Chad.

In light of these stories some questions arise, how does our culture teach us to deal with suffering? What strategies and attitudes are we taught in our early, developmental years in regards to suffering? Possibly the most important question is, are those strategies and attitudes the healthiest way to engage suffering as a human being?

I'm not going to lie, I grew up in a privileged situation. My father lived most of his early life in rural Arkansas. His family just barely scraped by financially, and at some point in the first third of his life he decided that he would climb out of that situation and provide a more financially secure life for his wife and children. His experience shaped his values. By the time I was born, Dad had completed a Masters degree and was President and CEO of a large, non-profit organization that sought to help and advocate for abused and neglected children. I am not sure how much money Dad made every year, but there were not many times in my childhood when I asked for something and did not get it.

We lived in a nice ranch style home with a big yard during the first years of my life. After fourth grade, though, we moved to a neighborhood about three miles away from that first home. The new neighborhood was bigger and nicer than my first neighborhood, and so were the houses. Everything from the sod to the concrete to the pristine landscaping was different in this new neighborhood. I remember riding my bike at a young age in my old neighborhood and finding a used syringe on the ground. My parents explained to me the dangers of drugs and why I should not touch something like that if I found it again. The new neighborhood didn't have syringes on the ground. It's not that there weren't drugs in this new neighborhood, it's just that people hid them better.

As I grew I began to learn the rules of the new neighborhood. For example, you always had to come across as having it all together. When people looked at your family you wanted to make sure that what they saw was put together and impressive. When you were back in your own house with the doors and windows closed then you could act any way you wanted, but you always had to be on your best behavior around others. Which leads to the inevitable question, why? Maybe it was connected to Dad's experience growing up and how he wanted to escape the life of poverty he knew so well. Maybe my parents' identity was wrapped up too much in what others thought. Whatever it was, I learned very quickly how to live and operate in a situation of privilege.

What I did not realize until later in life was that those values I embraced within my privileged upbringing began to affect all the ways in which I viewed and interacted with the world. I began to think that my comfort was of utmost importance. I even embraced the attitude that my whole life should be oriented towards providing myself and my future family with greater and greater levels of comfort. So, the thought of college became less of a place to learn and question and expand my mind, and instead it became the means for me to get a higher paying job so I could be comfortable.

This led to a very individualistic way of seeing the world. A majority of the time I would think about and only consider my needs and interests; this individualism was in line with what I learned growing up. If the goal of life was to further my comfort, then considering the needs of others was only a periphery concern that I would address after my wants and desires were satiated.

I was not alone in these values. I was surrounded by a culture that encouraged me to embrace them. Whether it was through media, or cultural stories, or even idioms and phrases, the world I lived in encouraged my values of individualistic, comfort-focused living.

Later on in life I realized that these values were not simply confined to certain aspects of my life, but that they saturated every part of my thinking and worldview. Clarity began to set in as I realized that these values even influenced the way I was taught to suffer, and although not everyone experienced the socio-economic reality in their formative years that I did, I came to find that these same strategies and attitudes were embraced by many within our privileged culture. We cannot escape the reality that we live in one of the wealthiest countries in the world,[4] and whether we like it or not (as I found out in my early years) certain values come to shape us as a result of our cultural setting.

So, how do the values of our privileged culture shape us when it comes to suffering? There are two main strategies of suffering that I see perpetuated and embraced across our culture: 1) avoid/numb suffering at all costs, and 2) individually internalize our suffering so that no one else can see it. Perhaps these invite further reflection.

How does our culture promote the strategy of avoiding/numbing suffering at all costs? Maybe a brief philosophical reflection on the facial tissue will help.

In our culture, when someone is crying we often look around for a tissue. When we find a tissue we hand it to them. Why do we do this? What is the purpose of handing someone a tissue while they are crying? The tissue is made of a very thin paper/fiber based material that absorbs liquids. So, the person who is crying can use it to soak up tears as well as to blow their nose. Both of these actions help to clean up the visible effects of crying. The goal for most of us when we hand someone a tissue is that it will give them the chance to clean up their tears and slow down their crying. Since crying is the outward expression of an inner turmoil, when we hand someone a tissue with the hope of slowing or stopping their crying what are we really saying to them?

Crying, then, often becomes something to avoid in our culture. When we begin crying we instinctively reach for a tissue. How many people have you seen begin to cry during a public speech in which they then apologize for their public display of emotion or follow with a phrase like, "I told myself I wouldn't cry." When did expressing our suffering and emotions become so taboo?

---

4. The fact that we can read this sentence emphasizes the resources and education we have had available to us that many in the world do not have access to. See http://www.uis.unesco.org for more information along these lines.

I have heard some say that they hand tissues to crying people so that those who are crying can "preserve their dignity in a public setting." That phrase is even more troubling. When did crying become an embarrassing action in our culture, an action that took away someone's dignity? Crying is a natural, human response to certain situations and feelings. For a whole culture to say that crying is unwelcome is to say that our natural, human responses are unacceptable. We are taught at a very early age to not just wipe away our tears and stop crying, but to wipe away our feelings in moments of despair and suffering. So, when we do suffer we try very hard not to express it. We put on happy faces, and if there are tears we go to the bathroom and "clean" ourselves up before others notice. We must look like we have it all together.

This discomfort with crying became evident to me when I first became a father. When my wife and I had our first daughter we were very excited for this new adventure of parenting. We wanted to be the best parents we could be because we loved that little bundle so much. Because I viewed crying as a negative action that needed to be stopped I associated our brand new baby's tears with something drastically wrong. The moment I heard her crying I would jump up and start to try to figure out what was wrong and how I could fix it. The problem was that her crying was not always as negative a response as I thought it was. Yes, babies do cry when they are hungry or uncomfortable or need a new diaper, but they also cry because that is the only way they know how to express themselves. I remember with great clarity the moment when another parent told me, "Chris, you don't have to freak out every time she cries. That's the only way she knows how to communicate." Eventually, I learned to respond to her crying not with panic and the desire to "fix" what was wrong, but instead with attentiveness. I didn't need to fix her when she cried, I just needed to be present and attuned to her needs.

Popular media also perpetuates this value of avoiding/numbing suffering. Take, for example, the thirty minute sitcom, or, if you are so fortunate, Saturday morning kids' shows.[5] If you subtract the show introduction, commercials, and ending credits you are left with somewhere around twenty-two minutes of plot developing show. So, in just over twenty minutes a crisis is introduced, the main characters respond to the crisis, and by the last couple of minutes the crisis is resolved and

---

5. I first heard Aaron Moore reflect on this during a visit to Monmouth College. So good, Aaron!

everyone walks away happy. As the audience, our emotions have gone from neutral, to engaging the narrative crisis, to resolution in just under the time it took me to cook dinner tonight. As enjoyable as this narrative television experience is, it begs the question, does the thirty minute sitcom experience resemble anyone's life that you have ever met? Outside of middle school dating relationships, do any crises in our lives reach their greatest intensity and find resolution in just over twenty minutes? The problem arises when we watch so many sitcoms throughout our life that we actually begin to believe, whether consciously or subconsciously, that our suffering can resolve itself in 18–20 minutes. We start to expect that recovery will happen almost instantaneously, and when it doesn't, we begin to wonder what is wrong with us.

In the sitcom world, suffering is a momentary inconvenience that can be glossed over in a relatively short period of time, and a resolution is guaranteed if we can only wait through a couple more commercials. There are almost no lingering effects from the suffering encountered by the main characters; life continues on in the next show without even a pause of reflection for the suffering encountered in the previous show. In our world, suffering doesn't go away so conveniently. Even minor setbacks that cause us minimal grief often distract us for a couple of hours or even a whole day, quite a bit more than the twenty-two minutes in the sitcom world. When moments of intense suffering come upon us resolution is not guaranteed, and the effects of our experience can stay with us for years. I have known many people who have wept months later because of suffering that had not been resolved. A sitcom like that wouldn't make it past the pilot episode. The reality of our lives is that healing sometimes takes a long time, and unless we understand that then we will often seek to avoid or numb our suffering when it doesn't go away in a short period of time.

There is also a sense of entitlement in our culture that encourages us to avoid/numb suffering. Whether it is our wealth or our perceived power, we feel that we deserve a life filled with happiness as we define it. If something goes wrong we can surely fix it with our abundant resources or position of prestige. Like the Queen of Hearts in Alice In Wonderland, we walk around with our chins up in the air knowing that whatever we want we deserve. This entitlement paralyzes our being when suffering enters our story. So, in response we do what those with perceived power do when something does not go their way, we seek to regain control of the situation. We either find distractions that keep our focus away from our suffering, or we find a way to numb ourselves so that we do not have to experience the uncomfortable effects of our pain. I have known people who have used cocaine, marijuana, and alcohol to numb their pain, and I have also known people who have used caffeine, food, and television to numb their pain. The length of the numbness does not matter, the quality of the numbness does.

These are just a few of the ways in which our culture encourages and teaches us to avoid and numb our suffering, but this isn't the only strategy perpetuated in our culture.

The other strategy that is encouraged is to individually internalize our suffering so that no one else can enter our dark reality. This seems like a natural response in a culture where the values of capitalism have had such a large and lasting influence.[6] Adam Smith, the grandfather of modern-day capitalism, summarized the inherent value of capitalism like this:

> It is not from the benevolence of the butcher, the brewer, or the baker, that we expect our dinner, but from their regard to their own interest. We address ourselves, not to their humanity but to their self-love, and never talk to them of our own necessities but of their advantages.[7]

Smith feels that it is the appeal to self-preservation that ultimately makes capitalism such a promising economic system. According to Smith, people are best motivated by self-preservation and self-interest, and America's economic system has been organized around those values for generations. Despite the many debates over Smith's economic proposals, what is evident is that when a culture organizes itself around these values, it will affect more than just one's economics.

Take some of our culture's phrases for instance. It was during the generation surrounding the Great Depression that the phrase, "Pull yourself up by your own bootstraps," came to be used more widely. For those who lost not just money, but their entire livelihood in the financial crash of 1929, the overwhelming advice they received was that if they were going to make it through their personal crisis they would have to

---

6. In this statement and what follows it should be noted that I am not anti-capitalist. I just seek to be critically self-aware of how our shared cultural values affect us as human beings.

7. Smith, *An Inquiry Into the Nature and Causes of the Wealth of Nations*.

do it themselves. This phrase morphed through the years but continues to communicate the same thing in our day, "You get yours, I'll get mine." The sense that my needs and livelihood are solely dependent on my individualism is one of the inherent values of capitalism that has shaped our society.

One side effect of this individualistic mindset is that my dependency on others is recognized less and less. I have seen this evidenced most clearly in regards to the grocery store. Numerous times I have asked young children about where their food originates. Many of these young children, especially those in an urban setting, communicate to me that their food comes from the grocery store. There is no concept in these young minds that we are dependent upon the hard work of the farmer, the harvester, and all those responsible for getting the food from the soil, to the store, to our plate. Food, one of our most basic necessities, demands our dependence on a whole variety of people; a dependence that is somehow disconnected in the minds of many young children.

This individualistic mindset combined with the language of self-preservation when rehearsed enough through media and commerce begins to shape even our view of suffering. Our suffering becomes a very individual experience that we seek to get through on our own. This is often due to a bloated sense of pride thanks to the lie in our privileged culture that we should have it "all together at all times." We view emotional response to suffering as weakness, and that is simply unacceptable to our inflated egos. This response fits well with the values of our culture that we are taught from an early age. We even applaud and praise those who make it through great suffering without the aid of others. We say that they made it through their suffering because they were "strong" or "determined" human beings. We pat them on the back and hope that someday we could be that strong. However, what is reflected on less is the reality that for every individual that seemingly makes it through their dark night by themselves, there are literally dozens of others who are suffering alone and will not make it to a place of healing and hope.

Are these strategies of avoiding/numbing and internally individualizing our suffering really the best way to engage suffering as a human being? As I journeyed through my suffering following the death of my parents, and as I encountered other stories of suffering, including the Judeans' story, I began to realize that there is another way, and that other way just seems more naturally and authentically human.

There is a common thread to the story of my parents' death, the Judeans' story of exile, and all of the stories of suffering that began this chapter. Despite the different circumstances that surround each story, despite the intensity or longevity of the suffering, what all of those stories have in common is a way of engaging suffering that subverts our culture's typical strategies. This way of engaging could be called *suffering with*, because in the midst of the pain and dark reality of the different situations, these sufferers chose to invite others into their suffering. This way of engaging their suffering was not a quick fix; life did not get better overnight. There was no 7-step plan to follow so everything would get better quickly. As time passed, though, they learned that hope could actually be found in and through the communities of people that surrounded them.

Suffering with looks very different than the strategies of suffering perpetuated by our culture. A brief look at the values of *suffering with* will highlight the inherent differences.

Nobody enjoys pain and heartache. No one hopes when they wake up in the morning that they will experience life changing suffering this day. So, it is not surprising, especially with the cultural values discussed above, that we seek to avoid/numb our suffering. Just like when a child touches a hot pan on the stove, we have learned to jerk ourselves away from the pain caused by suffering. However, the experience of inviting others into our suffering actually gives new perspective to the pain we experience in suffering. Instead of feeling isolated and alone we will see that we are surrounded by others who are willing to walk with us and support us through our darkest moments. When that occurs suffering becomes less of an enemy to be defeated. We can stop fighting the deep pain, and allow the gentle embrace of those around us to guide us through the suffering. Just as Jeremiah encourages the exiles, we can learn to be fully present in our suffering, and like Viktor Frankl, we begin to see that running from our suffering will do nothing good. With others holding our hands we can enter into our suffering to experience it for what it is.

It is this honest entering into our suffering with others where we can actually learn to embrace our suffering. What a strange phrase. Embracing our suffering sounds a bit masochistic, but once we realize that suffering is a natural part of being human in a broken world we can have the courage to embrace it as a piece of our story. Embracing our suffering can only happen, though, when we are surrounded by a community of support and love. This is the foundation for Alcoholics Anonymous and all subsequent recovery movements. At A.A. you embrace the reality that you are an alcoholic, with the hope that by embracing that reality in the midst of a loving community you can then walk through your suffering into a place of recovery and renewed hope. Any recovery movement will tell you that denial will not bring about healing or recovery; it is no different with our suffering, denying the pain of our suffering will only lead to further wounds down the road. It is only through embracing the reality of the circumstances while surrounded by a supportive community that healing and recovery can begin. This is the heart of *suffering with*.

Once others have been invited into the dark places of our suffering we come to realizations that are quite different than what we expected. The process of journeying from despair to renewed hope may take weeks or months or years. Rarely is healing and hope found in quick fixes. We live in a culture of quick fixes, instant gratification, and minute rice; but the journey through deep suffering is often long and arduous. It sometimes is an endless cycle of revisiting painful memories again and again. That thought is overwhelming and crushing when reflected upon in the midst of our rampant individualism. It is not as overwhelming, though, when surrounded by others who have committed to being present no matter how long the healing takes. When surrounded by others we can allow our grief to move at the pace it needs to, not at some false, hurried pace that others expect us to follow.

We are then freed to express our true emotions. When we invite others into our suffering we are saying "No" to the false masks we put up to hide our pain and brokenness. We live in a culture of "fine," a culture that expects us to look our best at all times. We lie and tell people we are "fine" when they ask how we are doing, but in reality much more is going on beneath the surface. It is the presence of others in the midst of our suffering that gives us both the courage and the freedom to express the real emotions that need expressed. If we do not express those emotions in a healthy way with others who have entered into our suffering, then they will come out in another, more harmful way in the future. Unexpressed emotion could emerge in physical ailments like ulcers or more holistic, psychological ailments like depression.

Take, for example, the difference between a Middle Eastern funeral procession and a typical American funeral. The videos and images I have seen of a Middle Eastern funeral procession show a large crowd surrounding a casket that is either being carried by the people or another form of transportation. What is fascinating to see, though, is the emotional response from the crowd surrounding the casket. People are wailing, crying, screaming. The look on the faces of the mourners communicate that nothing else in the world matters in that moment except their grief and suffering, and nothing will stop their expression of that grief. All of the American funerals I have attended, including my parents' funeral, are somber, quiet experiences. Of course there is crying and emotional expression, but that emotional expression is not supposed to interfere with the service being conducted. It is almost as if there is an unspoken rule about the level of emotional expression that is acceptable at a funeral, and of all the funerals I have attended, that rule has been observed.

Now, I understand that different cultures grieve in different ways, and that one culture's way of grieving isn't necessarily better than another. But I often wonder, how many people at those funerals I have attended felt inside like their Middle Eastern brothers or sisters, but did not feel the freedom to express their deep sadness in the moment because of unspoken rules? *Suffering with* allows for the natural expression of grief to find its way out of those suffering, and into the hands and ears of those surrounding the mourner. When that happens the fragile sufferer can be embraced in all of their emotions and thoughts.

There is a bereavement tradition within the Jewish culture that demonstrates well the values of *suffering with*. When someone experiences the death of a parent, spouse, sibling, or child the first stage of their grief is called *shiva*. This term refers to the significance of the first seven days following the death of the loved one. During this period, those who are grieving stay in their home while their community of friends comes to them. This community provides meals, takes care of any chores around the home, but most importantly is simply present with those who are suffering. An important rule that is followed when practicing *shiva* is that those who come to visit do not speak unless spoken to by those suffering. Not only does this prevent the awkward, and often destructive, attempt to say something of meaning to those suffering, but it emphasizes that it is simply the presence of the community that is enough to sustain in our darkest moments. Not words, not brilliant advice, not clichés, just the loving, sustaining presence of others who are committed to sitting in and walking through the suffering alongside of the broken.[8]

What if instead of avoiding/numbing or internally individualizing our suffering we chose to enter into it while surrounded by a community of people who were invited in? How would that change not just our experience of suffering but also our perspective on suffering?

Something happens in our perspective of suffering when instead of running from it we choose to enter into it with others. Jeremiah, and the Babylonian exiles, realized this. As was pointed out earlier, the devastating reality of the exilic experience would be enough for anyone to give up. However, it was into this dark reality that the exiles learned that their suffering, instead of being the end of their story, actually became the birthplace of something new.[9] It allowed them to imagine a life, both personally and communally, outside of their dehumanizing institutions. A life re-centered along the embodiment of divine philanthropy that called their nation into existence in the first place. In other words, Jeremiah's encouragement to practice communal living in the midst of their suffering allowed their experience in Babylon to actually form them positively.

My family and I have attempted to garden (and I do mean attempted) for the past four years. The experience has been a blast for both my wife and I and our three kids, not to mention that we could never go back to store bought tomatoes again. We learned early on that one important component to a healthy garden is the compost pile. Without good compost the plants will not get the nutrients they need to grow as healthy as they possibly can.

There are a variety of ways to compost, but no matter which way you do it the basic principles are the same. You need soil, moisture, heat, and a good amount of dead, decaying material. This dead material should be a good mixture of brown material (grass clippings, leaves, sticks) and green material (unused fruit and vegetable produce). When you mix it all together and give it enough time, the decaying process actually produces

---

8. An easy to read article explaining this concept was written by Lori Palatnik and can be found at http://www.aish.com/jl/l/dam/48958936.html#sittingshiva.

9. No one captures this idea better than Rob Bell in his book *Drops Like Stars*.

the most nutrient filled soil to aid the growth of plants in a garden. How strange? Remove any of the ingredients from the compost pile, though, and it will not work.

When we learn to enter into our suffering with others it is almost as if the same process of decaying and dying that happens in the compost pile happens within us. When we suffer pieces of us can die in the process. We may have lost something or someone that we will never have back again. But just like the compost pile, when we grieve well by allowing others to enter into our suffering, that very suffering that caused us so much pain can actually make us more alive than ever. Our suffering can actually shape us into people of hope, and hope is what a broken world so desperately needs.

Movement 3

A New Song to Sing

Standing on a hill in Galilee Jesus said to his disciples, "Blessed are those who mourn, for they shall be comforted." Blessings to those who mourn, cheers to those who weep, hail to those whose eyes are filled with tears, hats off to those who suffer, bottoms up to the grieving. How strange, how incredibly strange!

When you and I are left to our own devices, it's the smiling successful ones of the world that we cheer. "Hail to the victors." The histories we write of the odyssey of humanity on earth are the stories of the exulting ones – the nations that won in battle, the businesses that defeated their competition, the explorers who found a pass to the Pacific, the scientist whose theories proved correct, the athletes who came in first, the politicians who won their campaigns. We turn away from the crying ones of the world. Our photographers tell us to smile.

"Blessed are those who mourn." What can it mean? One can understand why Jesus hails those who hunger and thirst for righteousness, why he hails the merciful, why he hails the pure in heart, why he hails the peacemakers, why he hails those who endure under persecution. These are the qualities of character which belong to the life of the kingdom. But why does he hail the mourners of the world? Why cheer tears? It must be that mourning is also a quality of character that belongs to the life of his realm.

Who then are the mourners? The mourners are those who have caught a glimpse of God's new day, who ache with all their being for that day's coming, and who break out into tears when confronted with its absence. They are the ones who realize that in God's realm of peace there is no one blind and who ache whenever they see someone unseeing. They are the ones who realize that in God's realm there is no one hungry and who ache whenever they see someone starving. They are the ones who realize that in God's realm there is no one falsely accused and who ache whenever they see someone imprisoned unjustly. They are the ones who realize that in God's realm there is no one who fails to see God and who ache whenever they see someone unbelieving. They are the ones who realize that in God's realm there is no one who suffers oppression and who ache whenever they see someone beat down. They are the ones who realize that in God's realm there is no one without dignity and who ache whenever they see someone treated with indignity. *They are the ones that realize that in God's realm of peace there is neither death nor tears and who ache whenever they see someone crying tears over death. The mourners are aching visionaries.*

Such people Jesus blesses; he hails them, he praises them, he salutes them. And he gives them the promise that the new day for whose absence they ache will come. They will be comforted.

The Stoics of antiquity said: Be calm. Disengage yourself. Neither laugh nor weep. Jesus says: Be open to the wounds of the world. Mourn humanity's mourning, weep over humanity's weeping, be wounded by humanity's wounds, be in agony over humanity's agony. But do so in the good cheer that a day of peace is coming.[1]

---

1. Wolterstorff, *Lament For a Son*, 84–86.

6

Hope Arising

"Every time a host allows himself to be influenced by his guest he takes a risk not knowing how they will affect his life. But it is exactly in common searches and shared risks that new ideas are born, that new visions reveal themselves and that new roads become visible."

—Henri Nouwen

Another dusk has fallen, suffocating any light from the sun that had hoped to illuminate the world around me. Physically, I am alone in my dorm room. Drew, along with our good friend Heather, said goodnight to me about an hour ago. Mentally and emotionally, though, I have lots of company. Perhaps it is the makeshift memorial I have set up on my dorm room desk, or perhaps it is just the arrival of nighttime, but it seems like an evening doesn't go by where I don't sit in this room and just think. That is when I get into problems, because the thoughts, like the nighttime sky, are mostly dark. I have learned over the past few weeks that there are about half a dozen people who I can call in moments like these and they will genuinely welcome the conversation. Those people have become lifelines for me when I find myself drowning in my dark dorm room.

Dave and Jeanne are two of those people. I met them my senior year in high school when I started dating their daughter, Christi. The first time I met Jeanne I had just broken my leg in our high school's homecoming football game. My friend Ryan and I had planned to go hang out at Christi's house after the game, and I wasn't going to let my newly broken leg stop me from seeing Christi. She was one of the few things in my world at the time that could make my entire being feel peaceful in the midst of the chaos of life. With Ryan's help I hobbled into their house on crutches and lay down on the living room couch, hoping to draw lots of sympathy from Christi. After a few moments Jeanne walked in the room and we talked for a while about football and school and life. From that moment forward Jeanne and I have always enjoyed our little chats. She actually became one of the few people I could trust when I needed advice or simply just wanted to vent, and her hospitality always made me feel like one of the family.

When my mom and dad died Dave and Jeanne embraced me like their own son. Their door was always open to me, and I spent many nights talking with Jeanne. She shared with me the story of how her first husband had been murdered. He was a police officer in St. Louis and was shot while responding to a burglary. Jeanne became one of the few people whose empathy I could trust, and also became one of the mother figures in my life I could turn to when I was in need.

So, I picked up the phone and dialed her number, because this was a night I needed the comfort only a mommy could give.

"Hello."

"Hi Jeanne, it's Chris," I was hoping that the tone of my voice would communicate how I was doing without having to explain.

"You don't sound too good sweetheart. Tell me how you're doing."

"I'm just kind of scared tonight. All of my friends went back to their rooms, and I'm sitting here alone. All I can think about is how much of my life Mom and Dad won't ever get to see. My desk is filled with pictures and stuffed animals and all of these items that remind me of good memories, but I'm not going to be able to have good memories with them anymore, and I can't stand that thought," by this point my tears have turned into weeping, and Jeanne just patiently, lovingly waits for my crying to slow before she speaks.

"Chris, I am so sorry. I am so sorry," there is great sincerity in her words that I trust. I expect her to continue talking, but she seems to just let those words stay suspended in the air. In the ensuing silence I hear much. I hear her concern; I hear her compassion; I hear her love for me.

After a few moments she speaks, "I know how you feel, Chris. I know that you can't see past this moment right now, and you're not supposed to. But you have to trust me when I tell you that even though your mom and dad won't be a part of your future good memoires, you will have good memories again. I promise, and I can say that because I've lived it."

Had Jeanne just been another person off the street I wouldn't have believed her, but I knew her story. I knew that she had to go identify her husband's body after he had been shot. I knew how that had crushed her being. I knew how hopeless she had felt. But I also knew that she now has a husband and four children. Most importantly, in the past year and a half that I have known her I have seen her smile and laugh thousands of times.

※ ※ ※

"Chris, why don't you step into my office for a moment." Coach Akers held out his arm guiding me through the door to his office. Along with being the defensive coordinator for our university's football team he was also the strength and conditioning coach, so his office was in the weight room. I had heard rumors when I first got to campus about guys not being able to walk down stairs after a leg workout with him, and I found out that those rumors were absolutely true.

There was an intimidating presence about Coach Akers when he was in a coaching role. He was a master at controlling the inflexion of his voice to communicate what he wanted to communicate. When he started talking about defensive schemes you could easily become confused and think that you were in a battle for your very life. He was an exceptional motivator.

Having a conversation with Coach Akers outside of football, though, was a different experience. There was a genuine compassion that lived within the strong, tough exterior of that man, and it was that compassion that I sensed in his voice when he invited me into his office. We both sat down and he continued.

"I have received a lot of calls over the past couple of weeks from teachers and administrators from your high school. They want to support you and your brother in any way that they can, and they have asked if they could collect money and send it to the university on your behalf to cover any fees that your scholarship doesn't cover. Unfortunately, because you are an NCAA athlete you are not allowed to receive funds of that nature. It would be a violation of NCAA rules and you would be ineligible." This news was quite humbling and overwhelming. I had some very good relationships with different teachers, coaches, and administrators at my school, and some of them were parents of my friends, but for them to collect money to send to me made me feel loved and cared for in an intensely tangible way. Even if I couldn't receive the money I was grateful that Coach Akers shared the story with me. It lifted my spirits that day to know that I had the support of those from my high school. Coach Akers then continued to speak.

"So, I've done some research, and I have decided that, with your permission, I am going to petition the NCAA to make an exception for you in this case. I will create a letter on your behalf explaining your circumstances. My hope is that they will take your situation into consideration and allow those funds to come to the university to be used in whatever way would benefit you the most. Is that o.k. with you?"

Tears began to well up in my eyes and I had that feeling you get when you have so much you want to say that you can't even find a single word to begin to express it.

"Yeah . . . that's amazing . . . yes, I'm o.k. with you doing that," the words fumbled out of my mouth. Then, in all of the overwhelming feelings I had a moment of clarity. I looked at Coach Akers, "Coach, thank you for doing all of that for me. Thank you." After I said that I noticed that my eyes weren't the only ones filling up with tears.

Coach Akers quickly stood up from his seat and responded, "You're welcome, Chris. Just let me know if you need anything else."

There was a good feeling inside of me the rest of the day, and even though that feeling seemed foreign and out of place, I welcomed it with open arms.

※ ※ ※

As long as I can remember I have had an affinity for nature. Looking back on my life it isn't very hard to see where that originated. Every summer of my childhood, as far back as my memories go, we took a family vacation. Those vacations were always camping trips to a variety of places in the United States and Canada. Sometime between seeing mountains, and oceans, and trees, and rocks, and a plethora of animals I began to feel at home in nature. There was a connection with the world that I began to feel and foster even when we would return home from our vacations. In middle school and high school I would often climb onto the roof of my house and sit for long periods of time, because when I looked up at the vast canvas of sky above me I felt calm no matter what chaos was waiting for me back on the ground.

One of those moments came after my freshman year in high school. My older brother was getting ready to leave for college and the thought of him being somewhere else other than home brought me some sadness. So, after he left I climbed onto my roof. It was quiet up there, and it provided the space I needed to reflect and grieve. I don't know how long I was up there, but when I came down I felt ready to face daily life without my brother sleeping in the room next to me every night.

Maybe this is why after my parents died I sought out places in nature to be quiet and reflect. If I could find the right spot then maybe for an hour or two I could find escape and relief from the unrelenting thoughts and emotions. At the same time, being in nature reminded me of the good memories I had with Mom and Dad, and those memories were the closest I could come to connecting with them again. The city where I went to college was quite a bit smaller than where I grew up, so finding good spots around the city was difficult. The parks weren't bad, but I longed for less public places like rooftops where I could find some genuine solitude.

One spring day I found a semi-secluded spot by the river that looked promising. Like most days my thoughts were heavy with reflection and memories, and a piece of me thought that the river may have some answers. So I sat and looked and listened. What caught my attention were the trees along the banks on each side of the river. They were so big that they seemed to form a tunnel for the river to pass through that almost looked magical. Then, I noticed the tiny dots of green all over their branches. They were beginning to bud, and something about that felt good. After a few moments of examining the little buds I noticed the great irony that was present in that moment. On the bank of the river closest to me I noticed a couple piles of old, dead leaves that must have dropped to the ground last fall. For one reason or another they were still there. Why they didn't get blown away or washed into the river I don't know. Here I was enjoying the mystery and beauty of new buds, and right below those branches laid the dead leaves that used to be nourished and supported on those very branches.

My mind went crazy. How is it that death and life are so interconnected in the world in which I live? Did the tree mourn when it let go of its old leaves the previous fall? Did it celebrate when the new buds began to form in the spring? Most importantly though, how could it go on producing new buds every spring knowing that death is their inevitable end just a few months later?

The trees never answered my questions, nor did the river, but the simple act of asking the questions was enough for me in that moment.

◆ ◆ ◆

I have always had a thing for words. Reading was a regular practice that I enjoyed growing up, despite the fact that at times I pretended to do my reading just to appease my mom so I could go outside and play. Journaling was an activity I enjoyed quite a bit too. There was excitement for me in having a blank page and being able to fill it with whatever words I chose in whatever order I wanted. Some find that same joy with paint or oil pastels or colored pencils, but for me it was words.

Poetry became an early love of mine. I don't know why I was drawn to poetry so early in my life. There was an aura and mystery about poetry that excited me like nothing else could. I would hang pieces of paper all around my room with lines of poetry or quotes so that I would see them on a regular basis. In moments of significance I would seek to capture it or reflect on it through writing poems. Like a kaleidoscope I could arrange the words in endless amounts of configurations expressing parts of me in creative ways.

It seemed natural, then, that I turned to words in my grief and suffering. I wrote and read poetry, read books centered on the themes of grieving and suffering, listened and analyzed song lyrics. I couldn't get enough words. Through all of these actions I hoped to find a bit of comfort and healing; at times I did, and other times I didn't.

The words I sought out were certainly helpful as I walked through my suffering, but the words that were most soothing came in the form of letters from other people. Every so often I would walk to my campus mail box and find an envelope from someone seeking to brighten my day. Some of the envelopes were cards and others were letters, but all in all they were successful in their original intent. Christi, who knew of my love for words more than anybody, came up with an amazing idea for my birthday. She contacted two dozen of my closest friends and asked them to write a letter to me describing why I was important to them. She then collected the letters and arranged them in a scrapbook with pictures to go along with all of the letters. When she presented the gift to me I was absolutely blown away. Page after page was filled with words of friendship, love, care, memories, and support. I could hear the voices of my friends narrating their letters as I read them, and somewhere in those words I felt a comfort greater than anything I had experienced since Mom and Dad died. Christi's gift of words nourished and healed me in ways that I couldn't even begin to describe.

Hazel, who had become my mom's best friend during the last few years of her life, also sent me cards and little gifts seeking to lift my spirit. A compassion resided within Hazel that made her someone you wanted to be around all the time, which is probably a lot of the reason why my family spent so much time with her while I was in high school. Most holidays included a time when we would get together with Hazel, either for a meal or simply just to sit and visit. It became a tradition I enjoyed. One of Hazel's children lived in town which meant that we saw them quite a bit during those holiday gatherings. We enjoyed our times together, and if a stranger had walked in on all of us they probably would have suspected that we were all related.

Hazel had another daughter whose name was Sharon, but she and her family lived in a different state, so we did not have much interaction with them. That is why it came as quite a surprise when I went to check my campus mailbox and found a card and letter from Sharon. Her words were gentle and comforting, almost motherly, and I was very grateful for the time she took to write to me. Like the other cards and letters I received I placed her card and letter in a box so that I could revisit her words in the future when I needed some comfort.

There was a pleasant surprise the next week when I went to my mailbox and found another letter from Sharon. This letter was very conversational even though I hadn't written her back, and I read this letter a little differently. I had assumed that the first letter was just going to be an isolated incident, so I read it in that light. It still held great significance to me, but I didn't expect to receive any more letters from Sharon. So, after I finished the second letter I went back and reread the first. Sending one card or letter is an incredibly gracious act, and I never grew tired of receiving these one-time gifts. But to send two or more expressed an intentionality that brought with it a different type of meaning. As days and weeks went by the cards and letters from Sharon kept pouring in. The letters progressed from a tone of comforting and encouraging to simply expressing day to day activities. It was amazing to me how the letters simply expressing day to day activities began to mean just as much, if not more, than the letters intended specifically to comfort. When Sharon would express in her letters the mundane happenings of her day I began to feel a part of those mundane happenings. When she would write about little life decisions that she made I felt included in those decisions because she was sharing them with me. Here was a woman whom I barely knew, and she was writing to me about her trees, and flowers, and the weather. I was welcomed into her life on a daily basis through her letters, and despite my lack of correspondence back, the letters kept coming. Sharon wanted to journey with me and invited me to journey with her through her letters, and I welcomed a journeying partner along the strange path I found myself. She also made it very clear that she valued me not because I wrote her back, but simply because she cared about me. I have heard people use the phrase, "That person helped carry my burden," but Sharon showed me what it looked like, by using words.

❖ ❖ ❖

Awaking from sleep these days is a strange experience. Sometimes my dreams take me to good places, so when I wake up and remember the reality of my life it feels like the dream world I just left was reality and this life is just a nightmare. I keep waiting for the moment when I will wake up back to life before Mom and Dad died, but it only takes about ten minutes for my mind to abandon that hope.

I am still wiping sleep from my eyes when the phone rings. I clumsily stumble across the room and pick it up.

"Hello."

"Hey Chris, it's Lee. Just had you on my mind last night and this morning and wanted to call to see how you were. How are classes?"

"They're o.k. I have a pretty light schedule this term, but sometimes I just don't feel like going. I get in a rut and all I do is sit in my room and think. Sometimes I don't even have the motivation to go to football workouts."

"I can only imagine what it must be like for you on a day to day basis. Just do what you can and allow those around you who care about you to help you along the way. You've got a lot of people on your side, Chris. And you know that you can call me anytime if you need to talk."

"Yeah, I know that, Lee. Thank you. How are the boys?" That question was more of an attempt to steer the conversation away from how I was doing than anything else. In the midst of Lee's response my mind wanders. I think about how difficult the mornings are for me. Awaking from sleep is one thing, but arising out of bed and onto my feet is something else. Most mornings I would rather just lie there than get up, so this morning I am grateful that Lee helped me to arise.

Glancing over at the clock I remember that I have a friend who is supposed to stop by my room in less than 30 minutes. I mention that to Lee and we wrap up our conversation. "Thanks for calling Lee, I needed it this morning."

"You're welcome. Take care and we'll talk soon." His familiar southern drawl reassures me that I can make it through this day. We hang up the phone and I walk down to the bathroom to try and wake myself up a bit more.

When I step back into my room I become aware of the putrid odor that has overtaken every corner of my dorm. My mind is rapidly trying to associate that smell with past experiences so I can figure out how to take care of it. All of a sudden I place it, it smells like a dead, decaying animal. I try, in my still a bit sleepy state, to brainstorm where the smell could be coming from, then it hits me. Drew had talked for a couple of weeks about getting a pet snake. Maybe he was inspired by the guy down the hall from me who kept a six foot python in his room unbeknownst to the RA who lived on the floor. A six foot python seemed like a bit much for Drew, so instead he decided to start small and bought a corn snake that was only about six inches long and named him Asaph. After a week of hiding it in his dorm room the RA found out about Drew's new pet and gave him one day to get rid of it before he got fined. So, the logical decision was to bring it up one floor to my room.

It has only been in my room for just over a day, but we hid it behind some furniture and I didn't even remember it was there until now. Yesterday Drew fed it a tiny, baby mouse, so the smell is probably related to that whole process of digestion. Whatever it is, it is overwhelming.

Just as I start opening the windows to get some fresh air I hear a knock on my door. I go over and open it up and invite Ed into my foul smelling room. Ed was the pastor at the church I grew up in during my middle school years. He and his family were hospitable in a way I had never experienced; as a result I felt a deep connection with their family. They embraced me in all of my middle school awkwardness, and that was something I didn't easily forget. He and his family moved away around the time when I started high school, and in an ironic twist they ended up settling in the city where I would eventually attend college. Ed and his family have been another strong support for me over the past few weeks and months since Mom and Dad's death. He called me a couple of days ago and offered to come visit me, that was an offer I gladly welcomed.

After only a few steps into my room I can tell that Ed is trying to figure out whether to acknowledge the smell or pretend it isn't there. Of course, this happens to be Ed's first time in my dorm room, so lord knows what he is thinking. I know that a guy's college dorm room, by definition, is supposed to emanate some level of unappealing odor, but this is over the top.

We begin to talk about school and football and suffering and grief. Ed reassures me of his support and his family's support. I talk for a bit about how I'm doing and what the past week has been like. Then, I walk Ed through the makeshift memorial I have set up on my desk. As I talk about each item and what it represents Ed listens with great empathy. His eyes communicate to me that although my pain is my own, he wants to respect and honor my pain to the greatest degree that he can.

In spite of the sincerity of his questions and the genuine concern he expresses, there is an elephant in the room, or more accurately a dead and decaying elephant in the room, that lingers over our conversation. I try to address it by timidly apologizing for the odor and expressing that I have no idea why it is so strong, but at the same time I have that feeling like I'm trying to hold back laughter during the whole conversation. It's nice to feel like I want to laugh again.

Ed and I wrap up our conversation and exchange words of thankfulness for the visit. Despite the brevity of the meeting I enjoyed seeing and talking with Ed. Moments like these remind me of the great community of people that are surrounding me in my present circumstances. That reminder will sustain me for at least half of a day, maybe longer.

As soon as Ed leaves I call Drew up to my room, because it would do no good to try to explain over the phone just how horrible it smells up here. He walks in and immediately pulls his shirt up over his nose, a gesture I'm sure Ed wanted to do the whole time he was visiting. Drew moves the furniture out of the way and sets the tank in the middle of the room. It takes us less then five seconds to confirm that the smell is coming from the tank. As I'm looking around for some big pile of snake excrement Drew pokes Asaph. Asaph doesn't move. After a couple more pokes we realize that the smell isn't coming from Asaph's digestive process, it's coming from Asaph who is clearly dead. Drew then realized that the baby mouse he fed Asaph yesterday was still frozen, and that is one of the easiest ways to kill a cold-blooded reptile. Now I imagine that an animal that small, in normal circumstances, wouldn't give off such a foul, rotting odor that quickly. I mean he's only been dead for less than 24 hours. The problem, though, is that to have a pet snake you have to have a heat lamp set up to mimic the warmth of the sun in their natural environment. So, Drew and I learned assuredly that day that a heat lamp speeds up the decaying process among dead corn snakes, and the smell of the dead animal increases exponentially with every second that passes.

※ ※ ※

It is a bright, blue day. A day when the grass and trees seem to respond to the sun's invitation of beauty, their luscious green invites all kinds of creatures to come out and play. Springtime days like this are longed for in the Midwest after months and months of gray, cloudy winter. Days like this remind us that winter's death grip doesn't last all year long... spring will eventually wake up and arise.

Typically, a day like this would mean that my spirit is naturally lifted. The air would taste more sweet, colors would feel more vivid, life would have an extra bounce in its step. But not on this bright, blue day. For some reason the beauty of this day only serves to illuminate the contrast within me. I don't feel bright or blue. Sunlight and green grass may be what surrounds me, but inside I see clouds and withered, brown, dried out grass.

On this day classes come and classes go. The past few months have taught me how to endure days like this: just survive. Go to class, get through it, and go to the next thing. Eat lunch, check e-mail, go to the bathroom, and if I'm lucky night will come soon so I can sleep and try again tomorrow.

After lunch I have a couple of hours until my next obligation. Today feels like a day when I will just stay in my room for those empty hours. That seems like the best choice, but the day seems to call to me from outside my room. It beckons me with its siren's song to come and wade in the beauty of the day. However, nature has always been a friend I can trust, and I have no reason to think that it will try to drown me today. So, I heed the call, grab one of my favorite poets, and tentatively leave my room.

Hope Arising

Despite my inner disposition I can't ignore that there is a liveliness on campus today that isn't always present. Frisbees are being thrown, laughter can be heard, skateboards and rollerblades usher people along walkways. There is a battle going on inside of me. I so desperately want to enjoy the beauty of the day, but something is telling me not to. I feel like a prisoner in my own sadness, and I don't even want to be sad today. I'd like to just live and laugh and maybe even throw a frisbee. So, in revolt against my captor I find an open space of grass and lay down with my book of poems.

The sun feels good on my skin. Its warmth is soothing. There is activity all around me, but in this space I feel still, I feel relaxed, I feel reflective. As I reflect I begin to acknowledge just how overwhelmed I am in this moment. I can't quite get my mind around the dichotomy that exists. It feels so good to lay in the beauty of this day, but inside there is still a sadness that the day hasn't driven out yet. Should I feel guilty for wanting to enjoy the day? That overwhelming feeling compels me to want to talk to God. So, I try. I express the dichotomy to God, and how I long to be able to just feel o.k. again. In a moment of naked vulnerability I tell it all. Tears are welling up as I finish, and then I wait. I wait for some response from the God who supposedly created the grass I lay in and the sun that warms me. Certainly, God will respond to me.

But God seems silent. I don't feel better or comforted or assured or anything. I'm laying here in my dichotomy and nothing has changed. I thought God responded to prayer. I thought God could be found when you seek. Where are you God? Whispers of disappointment, rather than God, echo in my head.

Instead I open my poems and begin to read, longing to find solace in their company. Ever since I can remember I have enjoyed poetry. I am drawn to the mysterious thing that happens when words on a page or in someone's mouth can evoke such deep emotion. How can words do that? I don't really have any intention in the poems I'm choosing to read now, I'm just reading and feeling.

Then it happens. That experience that the poet longs for as they write: I get lost in the words to such an extent that the poem becomes my voice, my words. I read and I read, the anticipation only grows. Something begins to churn within me. I understand this poem. I feel it. Its story and language resonate in deep places within me, places that haven't seen the light of day since Mom and Dad died.

The poem tells of a child and her father who are on a beach at night. They are watching the sky, seemingly enjoying the beauty of the stars and planets that shine above them. Then, a dark, black mass of clouds threaten to bury the stars and the planets. In response to the clouds the child responds:

> From the beach the child holding the hand of her father,
> Those burial-clouds that lower victorious soon to devour all, watching, silently weeps.
>
> Weep not, child,
> Weep not, my darling,
> With these kisses let me remove your tears,
> The ravening clouds shall not long be victorious,
> They shall not long possess the sky, they devour the stars only in apparition,
> Jupiter shall emerge, be patient, watch again another night, the Pleiades shall emerge.
> They are immortal, all those stars both silvery and golden shall shine out again,
> The great stars and the little ones shall shine out again, they endure,
> The vast immortal suns and the long-enduring pensive moons shall again shine.
>
> Then dearest child mournest thou only for Jupiter?
> Considerest thou alone the burial of the stars?
>
> Something there is,
> (With my lips soothing thee, adding I whisper,
> I give thee the first suggestion, the problem and indirection,)
> Something there is more immortal even than the stars,
> (Many the burials, many the days and nights, passing away,)
> Something that shall endure longer even than lustrous Jupiter,
> Longer than sun or any revolving satellite,
> Or the radiant sisters the Pleiades.[1]

The pattern of my breathing has slowed. As those lines of poetry continue to dance in my head I feel calm and almost, dare I say, peaceful. Clarity seems to overtake my thoughts as the words of the poem take their final bow. For the first time in months I feel a tinge of hope within my being. A sense that the suffering I am experiencing does not have

---

1. Walt Whitman, "On the Beach at Night," lines 14-32.

to have the final word in my life. Maybe the despair I have felt will one day dissipate. Maybe like the little girl in the poem I'm longing for God to take me by the hand and reassure me that the burial clouds will pass. Then, the clarity sharpens. As I look back over the past few months I realize that God has been holding my hand and reassuring me along the arduous path of my suffering. God's hand has been young, old, male, female, white, and black. God's voice reassuring me that the stars will arise again has come through the phone, through letters, and through multiple face to face interactions. I now understand that it is because of God's presence through all of those who have surrounded me that I am able to hear the hope within this poem. Those words mean something to me now, I can hear their hope, because of the community of people that have loved me and surrounded me.

My upbringing taught me that God was to be found in temples, and books, and once-a-week events that typically happen on Sunday morning. These were the places were God could be found. However, lying here in this grass I have become acutely aware that God could also be found in a group of people, in tears of sorrow, and even in the words of a 19th century poet. For reasons I can't explain God left the temples and books and once-a-week events to find me in my exile, in my suffering.

I arise from the field of grass and look around for a moment. This day seems less scary than it did just an hour ago. I welcome the sense of serenity that surrounds me and allow it to lead me forward through the rest of my day.

After completing the final obligations of the day I call Drew and meet him for dinner. We eat and talk and make plans to hang out with some friends later in the evening, an idea that earlier in the day I probably would have turned down, but now it actually seems enjoyable.

As I make my way back to my dorm room I realize that I really don't want to be in my room right now. For better or worse my room has become the place I've gone to in my darkest moments, and I'm afraid that if I go back into that space I'll end up sinking into thoughts and emotions that I don't want to embrace right now. So instead, I get in my car and go to a place I know is safe from the dark memories. Plus, since the sun is almost set I know that my destination will be mostly abandoned and I will be able to sit and think in solitude.

Once I park the car I climb the steps to the top and find a bench to sit. Even though this lake is human-made it still exudes the welcome that a natural body of water puts out. I sit quietly and watch the world around me enter into night. There is a stillness that overtakes the land, and even the steady sound of the nighttime crickets seem to further the stillness. I am invited into reflection, but this time the thought of reflection isn't as frightening as it has been the past few months.

I settle into my seat and begin to remember. Scenes that form the story of my life begin to play in my mind. Birthday parties as a kid where I could always count on the kitchen being consumed by decorations. Vacations to vast amounts of places: places we drove to, places that could only be visited by flying, places where we had to cross borders, places where memories were made that are as clear today as they were then. Moments of success where my family was there to celebrate with me: my first violin solo at a public concert, my first home run, winning the first grade spelling bee, my first touchdown, my high school graduation. For the first time since Mom and Dad died I am able to think of these memories without deep sadness coloring my thoughts. I even feel a bit of joy from these memories, joy that brings a smile to my face as I think about them.

Then, in a natural progression, I begin to think about my future. My entire being begins to brace itself for the impact of hurt and pain that typically accompanies these thoughts, but as I begin to imagine the not-yet-lived moments of my life the pain doesn't come in its usual force. I think about my wedding and future wife. I think about my children and what it will feel like to be a daddy someday. I imagine my vocational pursuits. A sense of surprise sets in as I continue to bask in these thoughts without the sharp feelings of loss taking over. I certainly still feel some sense of loss as I imagine my future without my parents, but the feeling of loss isn't crippling this time.

In response to the nascent strength I feel in my being I arise from the bench and walk towards a pier. Darkness has fully set in all around me, and yet I am not afraid. I step out onto the pier conscious of the feeling that I have left solid ground, now all that separates me from the dark abyss below are a couple of pieces of wood and metal. The darkness feels even more thick the further I step out onto the pier.

Then, I see it. The end of the pier is only about seven steps in front of me, and the closer to the edge I get the more unsteady the pier feels. It bobs up and down and side to side, my body just goes along for the ride. When I reach the edge I pause and look. Everything is dark, I can't make out ten feet in front of me let alone the bank on the other side. If I were to step right now I would be stepping into a vast, unknown darkness. I wouldn't know where my next step would land, and as far as I can tell I would just sink to the bottom. But something inside of me in this moment wants to step, wants to thrust myself into the dark unknown of what is ahead because for the first time in a long time I don't feel afraid. I take a foot and place it over the water.

When my brother was five years old he saw Itzhak Perlman play his violin on Sesame Street and was as mesmerized as a five year old could be by Perlman's artistry. He then begged Mom and Dad to let him learn how to play, and before he knew it he was in violin lessons. Three years later I celebrated my fifth birthday, and you'll never guess what instrument I wanted to start playing. So naturally, my parents enrolled me in violin lessons too. Perhaps my love and fascination of music was born in those early years of learning to play the violin, or maybe it happened gradually over the next 13 years of playing. Whenever it was, music became a language that I enjoyed hearing and speaking.

I have a couple of good friends in my life today that are equally fascinated by music. Three of them play the guitar. Benji mostly just messes around on it, but get him around a campfire and he's pretty dangerous. Tim is a little more serious and really enjoys perfecting his playing. I never get tired of listening to Tim play. Dan is just flat out sick. Not only does he play and write music for the acoustic guitar, he is currently studying classical guitar with some pretty elite teachers. Last time I heard him play I ended up begging him for more when he was done.

I, on the other hand, don't play guitar well. Too many strings and chords for me. However, a couple of years ago Tim and Benji taught me a four chord progression that I just absolutely love. Even though it's probably only equivalent to guitar kindergarten, I can't stop playing it. The way the chords sound and progress is so pure.

One day not too long ago I was sitting on my couch after a pretty hard day. I had all of these emotions pent up inside of me and really wanted to get them out, so I pulled out a guitar and started strumming. After a couple minutes of fooling around I played Tim and Benji's progression. It was just right. I experimented playing it different ways: fast, slow, soft, loud, with crescendos, and without. Eventually I found the perfect way of playing that echoed how I felt inside. So I played it over and over and over and over. I never got tired of playing those four chords, and the more I played them the more comforted I felt.

Then, I realized that the reason I kept playing that progression over and over is because it went together. It fit. It had a beginning, a middle, and an end. Each cord individually wasn't that impressive, but when you put them together they became a whole. After the final E major chord there was a sense of completion. The more I played the progression, the more tears were pulled from eyes.

There is a progression in life. A way of living that is in tune with God, the world, and other humans. A way of living that just feels right, that just fits. Sometimes we live within that progression and we know it, because life just feels right. The way we feel when we experience love from another. The way we feel when we give of ourselves and somebody else benefits. The days when we are able to rest and enjoy life without the heavy weight of to-do lists burdening our minds. The hope and laughter and tears that accompany weddings or births. The feeling of deep satisfaction after accomplishing a goal that took much time and effort. The joy of watching your child grow and blossom.

But what about the times when life doesn't feel right, when it doesn't fit? When the marriage ends in divorce. When the friendship is broken beyond repair. When the one you loved so dearly dies. When you work so hard and you fall short. When those with more power and influence knowingly take advantage of you. When you try and try and try but just can't get clean or sober. When hope seems like an impossible dream. In those moments it's as if the last chord, the chord that ties it all together, is missing. All we feel is a progression that is unfinished. We know something isn't right, we know that this is not how the story is supposed to end. Isn't that why we hurt so badly in our suffering? Life isn't supposed to go this way, and nobody has to teach us that. We know it deep in our bellies.

In the Christian tradition that final E major chord, the chord that ties all of life together, is the resurrection. The belief that when Jesus arose from the dead something changed in the world. That what has gone wrong with creation is being put back together through the person of Jesus, and that includes human beings. One day God will make everything right once again and death and despair will no longer be part of everyday life.

But that hasn't happened yet. For those of us who have experienced the death of a loved one, or any other experience that causes us to suffer, the last chord is still missing. We still feel like we are playing a progression that doesn't make sense, because it doesn't end the way we know it should. I see glimpses of the last chord all around me: trees that appear dead in winter coming alive again in spring, using dead and decaying compost to provide sustenance to living plants, every time someone forgives me and the relationship is restored, watching my body heal from cuts and wounds. However, these glimpses don't give me the sense of completion that I'm longing for.

This raises some questions for me. I have met and conversed with people who have been through unspeakable tragedies in their lives yet they have found a way to not only survive, but to enjoy life once again. How does hope exist when the last chord is missing? How is joy possible when the progression of life feels incomplete? How do we live a life of meaning in a world where the last chord is missing?

Maybe the answer lies in the question. Maybe the realization that the last chord is missing is actually a realization of hope. Maybe the *feeling* that there has to be more to this progression than death and despair is evidence in and of itself that the progression doesn't end with death and despair. Maybe the unwelcome hurt I feel in the depths of my suffering is exactly unwelcome because somewhere in my being I know it's not supposed to be this way, and perhaps giving voice to that reality is the most courageous, most hopeful thing I can do.

It is the presence of those around me who remind me of this on a constant basis. I hear their stories and see their resurrection-filled choices everyday, and somewhere in the midst of that I'm reminded that my suffering is real and it hurts but one day I will join my voice to the voices of billions and shout together, "Where, O death, is your victory? Where, O death, is your sting?"[2]

As I walk into Jason and Jennifer's home I am greeted with smiles and hugs. Their two young kids come barreling around the corner in reckless abandon. I squat down to greet them and huge smiles spread across their faces. I even manage to get a high five from the older brother. The evening sunlight pouring through the large living room windows illumi-

---

2. Hosea 13:14; 1 Corinthians 15:55.

nates the white walls all around us. This feels so good. For the first time in six months I feel like I am home.

Jason and Jennifer, who were a part of my home church, approached me a couple of weeks ago and told me that I was welcome to stay in their home as long as I needed during the summer months. They knew that I had no desire to live in my old house after classes were done. It sounded like an inviting offer, but how could I ask anybody to welcome me into their home and lives like that? They would have to sacrifice so much, and I didn't know how to respond. My uncertainty lasted all but 2 minutes when Jennifer said that Jason had already built me a closet in the basement, I couldn't say no after that.

Jason walks me downstairs and shows me my room. "This is all your space. The closet is in here, and you can store whatever you need at the bottom of it." Jason has never been one to express emotion, but as Jennifer walks in the room there are already tears in her eyes. She puts her arms around me the way a mother or an older sister would.

"I am so sorry that this happened to you, Chris, but you are here now and we are going to take care of you. This is your home for now. Our home is your home."

Never before in my life have I felt the way I feel right now. I have stayed in other people's homes. I have even been invited to stay for extended periods. But never have I been embraced and welcomed to this extent by people who barely know me. Jennifer lets go of me and wipes her eyes. Her and Jason turn and head upstairs to finish dinner preparations. Once they are gone I sit down on my new bed and look around. After taking in the beauty of the moment I lay back on the bed. It feels soft and safe. I begin to think about the past six months, as well as the weeks and months ahead. Scores of thoughts and memories flood my mind, but in this place they feel o.k. They don't overwhelm me, they don't scare me. Gratefulness wells up inside of me for Jason and Jennifer and for their home. I don't know what the next weeks and months hold for me. I still carry around so much hurt and pain and confusion. So many unanswered questions still exist within my mind, but I am not afraid. I am no longer afraid.

"Chris, dinner is ready."

I arise from the bed and walk toward the stairs. My family just called me for dinner.

7

Judah's New Song

"The great problem in the life of man is whether to trust, to have faith in God. The great problem in the life of God is whether to trust, to have faith in man."

—Abraham Joshua Heschel

WHAT IF THE JUDEAN exiles living in Babylon actually responded to the communal imperatives in Jeremiah's letter? What if they built homes, planted gardens, shared meals, celebrated marriages, and had children? Would their suffering be erased in light of these life giving events? Of course not, but I imagine that as time went on and they continued to organize their lives around those communal imperatives they would find themselves hurting a little bit less. Perhaps as the days and weeks and months passed they would actually begin to enjoy moments in their life once again, and even looked forward to events in the future.

Isn't that what suffering does at its very core? It robs us of the future we imagined, so anytime we think about tomorrow we are sad because tomorrow is now unknown. What we thought we could count on isn't there anymore, and that creates fear and uncertainty. Jeremiah's communal imperatives, though, gave the exiles events that had future outcomes. Planting a crop of wheat or a date palm tree means that at some point in the future you are going to harvest and prepare the food that was grown. Becoming pregnant means that in nine months your life is going to change. Getting engaged means that at some point in the relatively near future you are going to arrive at your wedding day where you will be joined with another person. These future events would have been crucial to the healing and grieving process for the exiles.

It should come as no surprise, then, that the very next section of literature in the book of Jeremiah following Jeremiah's letter in chapter 29 is a section that primarily sets forth a reimagined future; a future of hope, of restoration, of rescue from exile. Up until this point in the book words of judgment and loss have dominated the text, but as we will see, new words are about to emerge, a new song is about to be sung.

Jeremiah 30–33 is often referred to as the "Book of Consolation." The text found in those chapters not only passively consoles the sufferers, but also actively infuses them with words of hope. It includes sections of both dynamic poetry and compelling prose. Many scholars believe that this text was written sometime close to Babylon's final siege of Jerusalem in 587 BCE.[1] This was the second attack, and also the most destructive, in ten years on the city of Jerusalem. Chapters 30–33 perpetuate themes only scarcely seen up to this point in the literature. Those themes include restoration and renewal of life, but everything hangs on the theme of rescue from exile and return to the Judean's homeland.

As we peer into these chapters of hope more closely we need to keep a question towards the front of our minds: Why do these tangible words of hope emerge now in the text, directly after Jeremiah's letter of communal imperatives? This is the question raised by the text, and to continue to interact with Judah's story of suffering, this is the question that we must eventually ask.

❖ ❖ ❖

Jeremiah 30 begins with a familiar introduction that emphasizes the Yahwistic origins of the words that will follow, but the language quickly turns to phrases seldom heard in the book before now:

> This is the word that came to Jeremiah from Yahweh: "This is what Yahweh, the God of Israel says: 'Write in a book all the words I have spoken to you. The days are coming,' declares Yahweh, 'when I will bring my people Israel and Judah back from captivity and restore them to the land I gave their ancestors to possess,' says Yahweh."[2]

A new idea is introduced in these first sentences that is expounded in the chapters that follow. Exile and captivity will not be the Judeans' real-

---

1. Clements, *Jeremiah*, 178; Stulman, *Jeremiah*, 258.
2. Jeremiah 30:1–3.

ity forever; there is hope for their future. Yahweh will "bring the people back" and "restore" them, an idea communicated in the original Hebrew language by the same word: *shuv*.[3] This word becomes the fulcrum on which the entire plot swings from despair to hope.

Shuv is a very common word in the Hebrew Scriptures occurring 1075 times. Like many words in the Hebrew language it can have a variety of meanings. A closer look at some of the more frequent uses will help us better understand its use in Jeremiah 30–33.

One of the most common definitions of the verb *shuv* is to physically go back or return:

> After the treaty had been made at Beersheba, Abimelek and Phicol the commander of his forces returned (*shuv*) to the land of the Philistines.[4]
>
> At the end of forty days they returned (*shuv*) from exploring the land.[5]
>
> So Samuel went back (*shuv*) with Saul, and Saul worshipped Yahweh.[6]
>
> When Jehoshaphat king of Judah returned (*shuv*) safely to his palace in Jerusalem.[7]

In each of these examples *shuv* communicates that someone is physically returning or going back to a destination. The emphasis in this use is that somebody (or something) has left a place and has now turned around and gone back.

Another common definition of *shuv* is to restore to a previous state, this could be in a physical, emotional, or functional capacity:

> Within three days Pharaoh will lift up your head and restore (*shuv*) you to your position, and you will put Pharaoh's cup in his hand, just as you used to do when you were his cupbearer.[8]
>
> So Moses put his hand into his cloak, and when he took it out, the skin was leprous—it had become as white as snow. "Now put

---

3. *Shuv* is pronounced with a long u. Like shoe with a v at the end.
4. Genesis 21:32.
5. Numbers 13:25.
6. 1 Samuel 15:31.
7. 2 Chronicles 19:1.
8. Genesis 40:13.

it back into your cloak," he said. So Moses put his hand back into his cloak and when he took it out, it was restored (*shuv*), like the rest of his flesh.[9]

Oh, that salvation for Israel would come out of Zion! When God restores (*shuv*) his people, let Jacob rejoice and Israel be glad![10]

Let their flesh be renewed like a child's; let them be restored (*shuv*) as in the days of their youth.[11]

All of these examples tell of something existing in one way, experiencing a change, and then returning to the way it used to be. Even though they are different and seemingly unrelated examples they all share the common theme of returning to what they originally were.

The last, and most theologically rich, definition we will look at for *shuv* is when it is used to communicate a returning to God. This returning to God, or repenting, includes both individuals and communities, and always encompasses the entire human being (mind, body, and soul). There is also typically an assumption that when you return to God you are turning away from choices or actions that are contrary to the way of God:

When you are in distress and all these things have happened to you, then in later days you will return (*shuv*) to Yahweh your God and obey him.[12]

I have sought your face with all my heart; be gracious to me according to your promise. I have considered my ways and have turned (*shuv*) my steps to your statutes.[13]

I have swept away your offenses like a cloud, your sins like the morning mist. Return (*shuv*) to me, for I have redeemed you.[14]

Afterward the Israelites will return (*shuv*) and seek Yahweh their God and David their king.[15]

---

9. Exodus 4:6–7.
10. Psalm 53:7.
11. Job 33:25.
12. Deuteronomy 4:30.
13. Psalm 119:58–59.
14. Isaiah 44:22.
15. Hosea 3:5.

Throughout the Hebrew Bible this act of returning to God is expressed in both a positive and negative sense. At times the people of God are chastised because they did not return to God, and at times they are graciously invited to return to God.

As these examples illustrate, *shuv*, like many Hebrew words, is rich and multi-faceted. Within these three definitions, though, we can grasp a basic sense of the word. To *shuv* is, in a literal and figurative sense, to return or go back. It is no surprise then that this word occurs more frequently in the book of Jeremiah than in any other book within the Hebrew Scriptures. *Shuv* appears 115 times in the book of Jeremiah, more then 40 more times than the next closest book. The book of Jeremiah is truly a book about returning: returning from exile, returning to God, returning to wholeness after deep suffering.

The incredible depth and significance of the word *shuv* in the book of Jeremiah is nowhere more evident than in its use in the contrasting, yet beautifully intertwined, chapters of 3 and 31. Out of all of the chapters in the book of Jeremiah *shuv* occurs most frequently in these two chapters, and what is even more intriguing is that it occurs the exact same number of times in both chapters, nine. Any good author will tell you that observations like that are not simply coincidence, the author of this literature is trying to communicate something to the reader, and to fully grasp the Judean's story we must ask, what is the connection between these two chapters?

Chapter 3 falls within a literary section that encompasses chapters 2–6 and consists almost exclusively of poetry, but this isn't your everyday poetry. As a matter of fact you may want to put the kids to bed before reading it, because even in spite of our tamed down English translations the sexual overtones are quite prevalent.

This section sets forth the case for Judah's unfaithfulness, they had abandoned who Yahweh had called them to be. The dominant, and most disturbing, metaphor used within chapters 2 and 3 for the people of Judah is of an adulteress wife who waits on the side of the road for men to seduce as lovers. The metaphor is then taken to a whole new level when Yahweh calls his own people a whore and a prostitute. It is this metaphor that begins chapter 3:

> "But you have lived as a prostitute with many lovers
>   would you now return (*shuv*) to me?" declares Yahweh.
> "Look up to the barren heights and see.
>   Is there any place where you have not been ravished?

> By the roadside you sat waiting for lovers,
> > sat like a nomad in the desert.
> You have defiled the land
> > with your prostitution and wickedness."[16]

So, Yahweh, tell us how you really feel. This language leaves no room for question with regards to Judah's unfaithfulness. Judah's actions seem to cut right to the heart of Yahweh. Yahweh is described as a faithful husband longing to love his bride, but Judah will have none of it. In one of the few prose sections of chapters 2–6 Yahweh compares the unfaithfulness of the northern ten tribes with the unfaithfulness of Judah:

> "I thought that after she [the northern ten tribes] had done all of this she would return (*shuv*) to me but she did not (*shuv*), and her unfaithful sister Judah saw it.... In spite of all this, her unfaithful sister Judah did not return (*shuv*) to me with all her heart, but only in pretense," declares Yahweh.[17]

Yahweh is seemingly perplexed in this passage that the people did not turn around and seek the relationship and way of life that they once had with Yahweh. The language used in these texts does not portray a ruthless deity positioned for revenge. Rather, there is a longing that emerges in the written tone of these words, a longing for the people to come back, as if Yahweh's hopes have been crushed by their faithlessness to the covenant. This longing is repeatedly intensified in three similar uses of *shuv* in the second half of chapter 3:

> "Return (*shuv*), faithless Israel," declares Yahweh.[18]

> "Return (*shuv*), faithless people," declares Yahweh, "for I am your husband."[19]

> "Return (*shuv*), faithless people; I will heal your faithlessness."[20]

There is a sense within all of these uses of *shuv* that Yahweh is waiting with open arms for the people to return. Yahweh will welcome them back into the relationship even in spite of their promiscuity. If this were

---

16. Jeremiah 3:1b–2.
17. Jeremiah 3:7, 10.
18. Jeremiah 3:12.
19. Jeremiah 3:14.
20. Jeremiah 3:22.

a scene in a movie, would there be tears running down Yahweh's face during these lines?

As the text continues, however, we learn that the people don't return. They don't come back to their first love. Their self-centered lives continue to lead them further and further away from Yahweh and the way of living that Yahweh entreated. The result, everything they held dear was taken from them. They wanted a life without Yahweh and Yahweh gave it to them in the Babylonian invasion and exile, but as we will see Yahweh does not stop pursuing his bride, even after their divorce.

Fast forward now to the days of the exile. Jeremiah has recently implored them to participate in community building activities that will ground the exiles in formative practices, practices central to who they are as a people and who Yahweh is as their God, practices that will slowly heal the pain of their suffering. Then, the text of Jeremiah 30-33 enters their suffering reality and begins to interject a new future into their scarred imaginations.

Before we look at the connection between chapter 3 and 31 we must take a brief look at chapter 30. This text speaks of the restoration of Judah back to their land and to a more faithful way of living as Yahweh's people, but in an unexpected twist the text imagines not just Judah's restoration, but Israel's as well! The chapter begins like this, "These are the words Yahweh spoke concerning Israel and Judah."[21] Throughout the book of Jeremiah the terms Israel and Judah are used synonymously, but in this introduction it seems as if the author is distinguishing between the two. Perhaps Judah's restoration will also lead to the reconciliation of the two divided nations. By the end of chapter 30 restoration and hope seem like a possible reality. For the exiles who are living in a foreign land these words are a cool drink on a hot summer day, refreshing their entire beings as they realize that Yahweh has not abandoned the people.

Chapter 31 continues this poetry of hope through language of comfort and future restoration. After appearing five times in chapter 30, *shuv* shows up nine times in chapter 31, appearing primarily in the first half of the chapter. It is no doubt that a message of hope to a group of geographically dispersed people would include a message of return, but a close reading of this text points out the observation that the "return" spoken of in chapter 31 is so much more than just geographical, "So there is hope for your descendants," declares Yahweh. "Your children will re-

---

21. Jeremiah 30:4.

turn (*shuv*) to their own land."²² The children returning to the land is the reason there is hope. As we have noted throughout Judah's story, living in their land was supposed to contribute to their formation as Yahweh's people. It is no wonder that this author connects their return with a new, realized hope.

This returning is also directly linked to their intense suffering. One of the most potent expressions of suffering in the entire Hebrew Bible is found in this chapter:

> This is what Yahweh says:
> "A voice is heard in Ramah,
>   mourning and great weeping,
> Rachel weeping for her children
>   and refusing to be comforted
>   because they are no more."²³

Here, Rachel, who is an ancestral matriarch in the story of the Hebrew people, is weeping because her people are no more. They are gone. There is no comfort for Rachel, because how can a mother be comforted when her children have been taken far from her arms of safety? One tradition suggests that Ramah, which is a city five miles north of Jerusalem, served as the headquarters for departure during the Babylonian invasion. If this is true then the city referred to in this lament was one of the last cities the Judeans would see before they were deported to Babylon.²⁴ Out of this deep expression of suffering, Yahweh responds with these words:

> This is what Yahweh says:
> "Restrain your voice from weeping
>   and your eyes from tears,
> for your work will be rewarded,"
>   declares Yahweh.
> "They will return (*shuv*) from the land of the enemy.
> So there is hope for your descendants,"
>   declares Yahweh.
> "Your children will return (*shuv*) to their own land."²⁵

Returning, both literally to the land and figuratively to Yahweh, will be the place where hope begins to emerge out of their compost pile of

---

22. Jeremiah 31:18.
23. Jeremiah 31:15.
24. See Jeremiah 40:1–4.
25. Jeremiah 31:16–17.

suffering. Rachel may choose to never be comforted, but according to Yahweh, when the children return, hope will be born.

So the equal use of *shuv* links chapter 3 and chapter 31, but as we have seen their use is very different. In chapter 3 Yahweh pursues his adulteress wife and asks her to return. The people have left the place of faithful Yahwistic living, and they do not want go back. Yahweh continues to plead with them to return, yet for all of Yahweh's attempts Judah chooses their own path. By chapter 31 the people have been overcome with sorrow and suffering in light of the Babylonian invasion and exile. It is into this setting that Jeremiah wrote his letter instructing the people to participate in formative communal practices, so as not to forget their identity as Yahweh's people. Following this letter, chapter 31 speaks up with language of return, and in an ironic twist it is Yahweh, the rejected lover of chapter 3, who will bring the people back from exile. Returning to their land, their homes, their lives becomes the place where hope is born amidst their suffering.

This progression from chapter 3 to chapter 31 is furthered by another tremendous use of language in chapter 31. In chapter 3 the people are referred to in terms that express sexual infidelity. It is utterly shocking then, to say the least, to see that twice in chapter 31 Yahweh refers to the people as "Virgin Israel":

> I will build you up again,
> > and you, Virgin Israel, will be rebuilt.[26]

> Set up road signs;
> > put up guideposts.
> Take note of the highway,
> > the road that you take.
> Return, Virgin Israel,
> > return to your towns![27]

In Yahweh's world, *shuv*-ing is so serious that it can actually change someone's identity from a promiscuous infidel to a healed, restored, returned, and reconciled virgin. Instead of scarlet letters Yahweh restores, reconciles, and heals; verbs so desperately longed for by the suffering Judean exiles.

---

26. Jeremiah 31:4.
27. Jeremiah 31:21.

Jeremiah 32 is a story that takes place in the tenth year of the reign of Zedekiah king of Judah and the eighteenth year of the reign of Nebuchadnezzar the king of Babylon, sometime around 588 BCE. Chronologically, this story follows the events of chapters 37–39, but it is placed within these chapters of hope because of its overall theme.[28] It is vital to keep in mind that this is only approximately 6-7 years following Jeremiah's letter to the first group of Babylonian exiles.

The story begins with Jeremiah who finds himself imprisoned by the wish of Zedekiah. Jeremiah, as evident throughout the text, represents a dangerous voice to the powerful elite in Judah. So, Zedekiah did what any power hungry ruler does with a dangerous voice, he silenced it. While in prison Jeremiah again received instructions from Yahweh, except this time it was not about a message he was to proclaim.

Jeremiah is informed that his cousin, Hanamel, is going to come to him and ask for Jeremiah to buy a field in Anathoth, Jeremiah's home city which is about three miles northeast of Jerusalem. Hanamel does come to see Jeremiah and expresses that it is his duty to redeem and possess the property in Hanamel's place. Hanamel is referring to an ancient Hebrew law found within the Torah, the first five books of the Hebrew Bible:

> If anyone among you becomes poor and sells some of their property, their nearest relative is to come and redeem what they have sold. If, however, there is no one to redeem it for them but later on they prosper and acquire sufficient means to redeem it themselves, they are to determine the value for the years since they sold it and refund the balance to the one to whom they sold it; they can then go back to their own property. But if they do not acquire the means to repay, what was sold will remain in the possession of the buyer until the Year of Jubilee. It will be returned in the Jubilee, and they can then go back to their property.[29]

This law guaranteed that nobody who fell into financial hardship would lose everything they had. If they were in that danger then a relative would step in and buy their property until they acquired the means to regain possession of it. This was not supposed to be a means for gloating. This was not the time to treat your relative as less than you because they could

---

28. Stulman, *Jeremiah*, 275.
29. Leviticus 25:25–28.

not afford their land. This was a moment to save them by taking care of the land, even in their inability. If for some reason the original owner did not acquire enough stability to reclaim possession of the property then they just had to wait until the Year of Jubilee and it would be returned. The Year of Jubilee occurred every fiftieth year, and during that year family property would return to the original owners. This guaranteed that no family in the unified nation of Israel would remain in cyclical, generational poverty.

This is all well and good, but why was Hanamel asking Jeremiah to participate in this law? At this time the Babylonian army had already infiltrated the entire area, which included Anathoth. They were cutting off all food and resources to the city of Jerusalem, and it was only a matter of time before they breeched the city's walls and conquered the capital city for good. For the law to work as it was intended it required that the original owner will at some point in the future be able to regain possession of the land, either when they acquired the resources or during the Year of Jubilee. What was Hanamel thinking? Either Hanamel was trying to get a couple bucks out of his cousin before Babylon came in and wiped everything out, or Hanamel believed that his family would have a future in this land. If he believed that, then he should have gone and bought a lottery ticket as well.

In light of the divine prelude to the whole interaction Jeremiah chooses to purchase the field. He then offers a prayer to Yahweh that recounts the acts of rescue and grace throughout Israel's history. Despite the clear goodness of Yahweh to the people throughout their history, Jeremiah's prayer ends with an honest statement that sounds more like a doubt or question than a statement:

> See how the siege ramps are built up to take the city. Because of the sword, famine and plague, the city will be given into the hands of the Babylonians who are attacking it. What you said has happened, as you now see. And though the city will be given into the hands of the Babylonians, you, Sovereign Yahweh, say to me, "Buy the field with silver and have the transaction witnessed."[30]

Apparently, Yahweh is not offended or disturbed by Jeremiah's honesty.

As the rest of the story unfolds Yahweh reassures Jeremiah that despite the infidelity of the people of Judah, they will be restored. They will return to the land once again and live in the land that they call home. The

---

30. Jeremiah 32:24–25.

simple act of buying the field becomes an audacious, subversive statement of hope right in the midst of the most powerful army in the world. Chapter 32 ends with these words:

> This is what Yahweh says: "As I have brought all this great calamity on this people, so I will give them all the prosperity I have promised them. Once more fields will be bought in this land of which you say, 'It is a desolate waste, without people or animals, for it has been given into the hands of the Babylonians.' Fields will be bought for silver, and deeds will be signed, sealed and witnessed in the territory of Benjamin, in the villages around Jerusalem, in the towns of Judah and in the towns of the hill country, of the western foothills and of the Negev, because I will restore their fortunes," declares Yahweh.[31]

Nothing could bring more hope for an exiled Judean than to read these words and imagine this story. Not only does this story speak of their return from exile, but it also imagines Yahweh's presence once again infusing their lives with meaning and purpose. Despair and death will not have the final word for Judah. Like the exodus out of Egypt, Yahweh will deliver and restore the people, but as we will see, with freedom comes responsibility.

❖ ❖ ❖

Imagine taking a walk through the areas of Babylon populated with Judean exiles. What would we see? What would we hear? What if we took a stroll through their neighborhoods and homes a couple of weeks after they arrived in Babylon? I assume that a heavy despair would be present on their faces. Defeated would be an appropriate word to describe their posture and ambience. Women would pass us on the street and not even lift their eyes to acknowledge our presence, let alone greet us. Men may make eye contact, but it would be far from welcoming. It would be the look of a wounded, cornered animal, hopelessness and anger mixed together at the same time. If there were children they may not understand what has happened in the past month, but they would certainly pick up on the mood of the adults. Uncertainty would eventually sink into their little minds and affect them too in tangible ways.

Now, what if we went away and came back a couple of years later? What would we see? Would anything have changed?

---

31. Jeremiah 32:42–44.

Time certainly does have an effect on our experience and progression through our suffering, and the Judeans would be no exception. But we all know people who ended up in darker places years after their suffering began, for them time did not intrinsically make everything better. What would we see on this return trip to Babylon? If the exiles embraced the urgings of Jeremiah, then I imagine we would hear the sound of babies crying in nearby houses as we walked down the street. If it were a weekend then we may hear music and see dancing as people gather together around tables of food. If we were lucky we would see a newly married couple emerge from their new home with that newly married look in their eyes. Older men who barely knew each other for most of their lives would be talking and debating and joking with each other because they recently gave their children away to be married to one another. If we were really lucky we would pass a home where many people were gathered and a single voice could be heard through the window telling stories of Yahweh's love and care for their ancestors. That would be an amazing sight!

That would be amazing because just like you and me those exiles would have to make a choice. What voices are they going to listen to in the midst of their suffering and confusion? Are they going to listen to the voice that tells them to be vengefully angry about what has happened? The voice that pushes them closer and closer to violent rebellion. That voice wants their attention, and if they surround themselves with that voice long enough then they will actually begin to believe that it is the best way to live as a human being. The other voice they could listen to is the voice of their ancestors. That voice is a voice that calls them back to who they are at their very core. A people brought together as one nation by the God who created the universe so that they may participate in the healing and restoration of the entire cosmos.

I imagine that would be a very hard voice to hear while in exile. To be honest, if it were me I may choose the voice of anger and revenge, because who would really have the strength or energy to listen for the counter intuitive voice of love that originated in the story of their ancestors?

Perhaps this is why the very first lines of Jeremiah 30 remind this exiled group of people that they are part of a story that is bigger than themselves, "'The days are coming,' declares Yahweh, 'when I will bring my people Israel and Judah back from captivity and restore them to the land I gave their ancestors to possess,' says Yahweh."[32] The natural human reaction to suffering is to turn inward and only think of ourselves. That is a positive and necessary response to suffering. However, the problem arises when we allow that healthy self focus to turn into self obsession. To be a member of the nation that is Yahweh's people is, by definition, to live with an awareness that the world is not how Yahweh intended it to be, and also to be aware that Yahweh is using you to be part of the solution. You can't be a part of that solution when all you do is stare in a mirror. This is why a simple reference to the Israelite ancestors in chapter 30 holds so much significance in the ears of the exiles.

Yahweh's desire for this people to be who they were called to be is so intense that Yahweh, in one of the most familiar passages from the book of Jeremiah, chooses to make a new covenant with the people:

> "'The days are coming,' declares Yahweh,
>   'when I will make a new covenant
> with the house of Israel
>   and with the house of Judah.
> It will not be like the covenant
>   I made with their ancestors
> when I took them by the hand
>   to lead them out of Egypt,
> because they broke my covenant,
>   though I was a husband to them,'
>   declares Yahweh.
> 'This is the covenant I will make with the house of Israel
>   after that time,' declares Yahweh.
> 'I will put my law in their minds
>   and write it on their hearts.
> I will be their God
>   and they will be my people.
> No longer will they teach their neighbors,
>   or say to one another, "Know Yahweh,"
> because they will all know me,
>   from the least of them to the greatest,'
>   declares Yahweh.
> 'For I will forgive their wickedness
>   and will remember their sins no more.'"

In this declaration Yahweh acknowledges that the marriage that existed with the people is broken. That covenant is null and void, it has no worth

---

32. Jeremiah 30:3.

anymore. Yahweh even recounts the grace and faithfulness that was shown to the ancestors, even though it was rejected. However, Yahweh wants to get remarried, and in this new covenant there are some significant changes. No longer will Yahweh's instructions be something the people have to try and figure out how to follow. Instead, in the new covenant Yahweh's way of living will be written on the minds and hearts of Yahweh's people. In other words, living in tune with the way Yahweh desires will just come naturally. No longer will it feel forced or awkward.

The old covenant only brought sadness and despair as the people realized their failings, but the fact that Yahweh has spoken these words to the exiled people and proposed a new covenant is a reason to hope that things are going to change. Exile will not be the end of the story.

※ ※ ※

After taking a bit of time to peer into the text of Jeremiah 30–33 we must now revisit the question posed at the beginning of this chapter. Why do these intensely hopeful chapters appear directly after the letter where Jeremiah gives the exiles the communal imperatives? Another way of asking the same question is this, how did Jeremiah's instructions in chapter 29 prepare the people to hear and respond to the hope expressed in chapters 30–33?

If we recall the state of the nation of Judah in the first half of the book of Jeremiah we will remember that it was a troubled nation. First, a division had existed between the northern ten tribes and the southern two tribes that was never intended to exist. Israel and Judah were supposed to be one nation living together in a unified pursuit of becoming more the people that Yahweh wanted them to be in the world. The division between the two nations served as a macrocosm of what existed internally in each nation.

Second, in the first half of the book of Jeremiah Judah was an extremely fractured community of people. In chapter 7 we learned that those with power and resources were taking advantage of those who had less power and resources. Chapter 11 tells of the brokenness of the covenant, the people stopped living the way Yahweh desired for them to live. This explains the existence of the prevailing injustice described in chapter 7. Their national unity is challenged even more in chapter 18 when the election, being chosen by Yahweh to lead the restoration movement, is dismantled. At this point they are left wondering, "What even makes us a nation anymore?" The final blow to their unity is the removal of the king, and the exposure of the prevalent injustice due to the king's actions. All of this paints a very dismal picture of Judah. They are a broken, divided nation ready to topple.

What happened in exile, then, that made this people ready to hear a new song of hope right in the midst of their suffering? As we observed in Jeremiah's letter of chapter 29, the people basically had two choices. They either throw in the towel and decide to become full fledged citizens of the Babylonian Empire, or they embrace Jeremiah's communal imperatives and hold onto their distinctiveness as Yahweh's people. The more they observe the communal practices of building houses, gardening, marrying, having children, and seeking the peace of the city, the more they will be drawn together; the more they will experience a commonality in their deep suffering that they did not experience back home in Judah.

Could we make the observation, then, that their suffering actually saved them? That it brought them together in a way that they needed to experience if hope was going to be in their future? Can we also observe that their suffering did not just bring the people together, it also brought the people closer to Yahweh? Back in Judah everything was getting in the way of finding Yahweh, even the very structures created to facilitate interaction with Yahweh. In exile, however, in their suffering they found Yahweh in places they never imagined.

It was this experienced exilic unity and their reconciliation with Yahweh in Babylon that allowed the hope of chapters 30–33 to mean something to the people. Imagine if these words of hope were spoken earlier in the story. Maybe if they were spoken back in chapter 3, would they have had any significance in the hearts and minds of the people? The uncomfortable observation from the story of the sixth century Judeans is that suffering can actually become redemptive. This is uncomfortable because we live in a culture where we are told that suffering is only negative. However, the Judeans' exilic suffering actually saved the people from becoming a destructive force in the world. Through the incomprehensible grace of Yahweh they are renewed and restored in their exilic suffering.

Does this mean Yahweh caused every piece of their suffering that they experienced at the hands of the Babylonians so that they would eventually be restored? Absolutely not. Yahweh found no pleasure in their suffering. Although Yahweh interceded by arousing the Babylonians against the Judeans, the Babylonians clearly went beyond their divine mandate in their treatment of the Judeans.[33] Quite the contrary appears throughout the book. Yahweh *responds* and *reacts* to the Judeans' destructive choices and eventually to their suffering. Yahweh pleads with them to return to lives of faithfulness to the covenant, it is Judah that initially refuses the invitation. Yahweh gives them a choice, and they chose religion and injustice.

Instead, what the book does communicate is that this Yahweh has the ability to redeem suffering. Redemption is the process of taking something negative or broken and remaking it into something healed and hopeful. For the Judeans their suffering becomes the place where Yahweh enters with them and seeks their well being, their healing, their wholeness, their restoration. In the story of the Judeans of the sixth century BCE, Yahweh redeems them through their suffering, not from it. Hope is found as they invite one another into their suffering and experience the healing that comes through the presence of the community.

---

33. See Jeremiah 50–51 and a similar theme in Zechariah 1:15.

Conclusion

It was a Thursday. The day was winding down, and I was finishing up the last few tasks I had to complete before I called it a day. After completing those tasks I walked across my dorm room to get something out of the fridge, but I never made it to the fridge. The path to the other side of the room required that I pass in front of the mirror. The figure that appeared in that mirror did not have all black on that day, and that caused me to pause. For four months I wore all black every Thursday. It was my way of grieving the death of my parents, but on this Thursday I forgot. The truth was that I had just had a wonderful couple of days visiting with Christi, and the joy I experienced in our time together lasted that whole week. When I woke up Thursday morning, grief and despair were not the first thoughts to enter my mind.

Then, a couple of more months went by and I began to notice that the little things in life began to bring me joy once again: a sunrise, a good meal, a fun time with a friend. There were plenty of days of sadness and weeping mixed in too, but those days seemed to occur less and less. As I began to take a deeper look at myself I noticed that I was surrounded by a large group of people that loved me and chose to walk with me through my suffering. Those people nurtured me in ways that I could not even comprehend in the moment, but little by little those people led me forward on a path of healing and restoration. If it was not for Christi I probably would have dressed in black on that Thursday.

Two stories, two plots, two different groups of characters, but a couple of themes that seem to intersect. I hope that in offering my story side by side with the story of the Judeans some who read this book will end in a different place than where they began. I hope that those who are experiencing or have experienced deep suffering would choose to invite others into that suffering. That may take some work, because many of us have organized our lives in ways that keep people at a safe perimeter. If that is the case with you then I hope that something within these stories would push you over that uncomfortable ledge, and you find yourself falling safely into the arms of those who genuinely care about you.

I agree with Viktor Frankl, to be human is to suffer. I do not, however, agree with the dominant voices in our culture that suffering is to be avoided at all costs. I want to live and breathe and swim and go for walks with my wife and play with my kids and celebrate with friends and have those moments where you wish you could just push pause. The reality is that to live that life will mean that I suffer. I used to be afraid of suffering, but now I just look around at those who love me for who I am and I realize that like the Judeans I have been given a new song to sing.

May you, in your darkest moments find that you are not alone. May you invite others into your suffering, and out of that invitation may the God who led Judah out of exile give you a new song as well!

Acknowledgments

WANTING TO SAY SOMETHING is one thing, getting that something into a medium where many people can engage it is a whole other thing. The journey of these ideas from my mind to the written page was, like the driving premise of this book, a communal experience, and I would be amiss if I didn't acknowledge those who made this book possible. (It is inevitable that I will forget some unintentionally, you know who you are.)

Benji, you are a friend and a brother, a breath of fresh air in the chaos of life. You encouraged and inspired me with your words from the very beginning of this project till the very end. Thank you for journeying back into these scary places with me as I wrote. You can be my pretend editor anytime you want, just don't expect your cut to go up.

Drew, we have lived, loved, cried, and laughed together for over a decade. Your support during this project was more vital than you could imagine, even in the midst of your deep suffering. Thank you for always reminding me that the bravest thing I have is hope!

Oliver, your talent is overwhelming! I am so grateful to call you my brother.

To my teachers:

Louis, this work would not have been possible if you had not been my teacher. Thank you for teaching me how to read Jeremiah, and for passing on to me (and many others!) your excitement for this important text.

Gary, your knowledge, wisdom, and love has shaped me more than you could ever know! Keep on keeping on.

Richard, you have taught me and inspired me more times than you know in the past five years. Please keep writing and talking, we need to hear what you have to say.

To the many who read my writing and encouraged me at different times through the process, thank you!

To those I watched suffer during this journey: Kelly, Sue (every time I eat a cookie I will think of you), Scott, Zac, Lynsey, and Josh. My heart broke for you, and I pray that out of your suffering you may find healing. In your sadness, may you never feel like you have to cry alone.

Dave and Jeanne, thank you for your support, I love you a bunch. I wouldn't be who I am today without your presence, love and support!

Rodney, Kim, Emma, and Bryson, you are our family. Your love and support carried us through many dark places. I would not have finished this without all of you. Brennan, I am honored and blessed to call you my brother.

Thank you Ryan Hamilton for your verbal and tangible support, you were one of the first voices to push me forward.

Dean, you are an amazing person, and I am proud to call you my big brother. Your enthusiasm for this project kept me going.

Finally, Hannah, Maegan, and Isaiah, you are absolutely the most amazing children a daddy could ever ask for. Thank you for all of the notes and pictures you wrote on the dry erase board while I was working, without them it would have been a lot harder to write. You three kept me going in ways your beautiful, young minds could never understand. Your daddy loves you as big as the whole wide world!

Christi, we have spent almost half of our lives together. We have walked through moments of speechlessness and ecstasy as well as some of the darkest valleys two humans could traverse. Through it all though, there is no other person in the world I would rather have by my side than you. I am who I am today because of you. Without your support and care I would not have been able to make it through this project. I love you dearly.

Bibliography

Alcoholics Anonymous. Fourth Edition. New York City: Alcoholics Anonymous World Services, Inc., 2001.
Bell, Rob, *Drops Like Stars: A Few Thoughts on Creativity and Suffering*. Grand Rapids: Zondervan, 2009.
Benjamin, Don C., and Victor H. Matthews. *Old Testament Parallels: Laws and Stories from the Ancient Near East*. Fully Revised and Expanded Third Edition. Mahwah: Paulist Press, 2006.
Bright, John. *History of Israel*. Louisville: John Knox, 2000.
Clements, R. E. *Jeremiah: Interpretation*. Atlanta: John Knox Press, 1988.
Frankl, Viktor. *Man's Search For Meaning*. New York: Pocket Books, 1985.
Fretheim, Terence E. *The Suffering of God*. Philadelphia: Fortress Press, 1984.
———. *Jeremiah*. Macon: Smyth & Hewlys, 2002.
Geisel, Theodor Seuss. *Horton Hears a Who*. New York: Random House, 1954.
Heschel, Abraham. *The Prophets*. New York: Harper Collins, 2001.
Homer. *The Odyssey*. New York: Viking Penguin Inc., 1946.
Kraybill, Donald B, et al. *Amish Grace: How Forgiveness Transcended Tragedy*. San Fransisco: Jossey-Bass, 2007.
Linkin Park, "Easier to Run." *Meteora*. Warner Bros., 2003. CD.
Meier, Richard. "Synagogue." In *Encyclopedia Judaica* 15:579–80.
Middleton, J. Richard. *The Liberating Image: The Imago Dei in Genesis 1*. Grand Rapids: Brazos Press, 2005.
Middleton, J. Richard, and Brian Walsh. *The Transforming Vision: Shaping a Christian World View*. Downers Grove, IL: InterVarsity, 1984.
Silverstein, Shel. *The Giving Tree*. Evil Eye Music, Inc., 1964.
Smith, Adam. *An Inquiry Into the Nature and Causes of the Wealth of Nations*. London: Nelson & Sons, 1870.
Speiser, E. A. "The Creation Epic." In *The Ancient Near East: An Anthology of Texts and Pictures*, edited by James B. Pritchard, 31–39. London: Oxford University Press, 1958.
Stulman, Louis. *Jeremiah: Abingdon Old Testament Commentaries*. Nashville: Abingdon Press, 2005.
———. *Order Amid Chaos: Jeremiah as Symbolic Tapestry*. Sheffield: Sheffield Academic Press, 1998.
Whitman, Walt. "On the Beach at Night." In *Leaves of Grass*, 221–22. New York: Signet Classic, 2000.
Wolterstorff, Nicholas. *Lament for a Son*. Grand Rapids: Eerdmans, 1987.
Young, William P. *The Shack*. Los Angeles: Windblown Media, 2007.

Contact the Author

For 30 years Chris Williams has been living, laughing, loving, and crying, just like you. Eleven of those years have been spent with the four most important people in his life: his wife Christi and his children Hannah, Maegan, and Isaiah. He is compelled by the worldview of hope offered within the biblical story and longs to see that story taken out of the hands of those who manipulate it for selfish gain and placed into the hands of people like you and me. Chris would love to hear your story and welcomes further conversation. He can be reached at:

lifeaftersuffering@gmail.com

May the God who joins us in our suffering sustain and restore you in ways you never thought possible.

www.ingramcontent.com/pod-product-compliance
Lightning Source LLC
Chambersburg PA
CBHW051106160426
43193CB00010B/1342